MOMENTS WITH GOD
for Women

100 DEVOTIONS
FOR REFLECTION AND RENEWAL

Our Daily Bread
Publishing™

Moments with God for Women: 100 Devotions for Reflection and Renewal
© 2022 by Our Daily Bread Ministries

The devotional readings collected in this book were first published over a span of years in *Our Daily Bread* devotional booklets that are distributed around the world in more than fifty languages.

Interior design by Michael J. Williams

ISBN: 978-1-916718-00-5

Library of Congress Cataloging-in-Publication Data Available

Printed in Europe
22 23 24 25 26 27 28 29 / 8 7 6 5 4 3 2 1

INTRODUCTION

He got up, rebuked the wind and said to the waves, "Quiet!
Be still!" Then the wind died down
and it was completely calm.

Mark 4:39

Quiet, be still, Jesus said to the wind and the waves. And in the gospel of Matthew, we read that Jesus calls those listening to find peace in Him: *Come to me, all you who are weary and burdened, and I will give you rest* (11:28). Your Savior extends that invitation to you as well.

For the next hundred days, let Jesus's words, and His Word, anchor you to Him and the quiet rest He provides. No matter the storms in your external environment or within your own spirit—the fears, discouragements, and regrets that hijack your joy—you can find refuge meditating on God's love for you.

In *Moments with God for Women*, you'll have the opportunity to pause. Quiet yourself. Connect with God. Whether you choose to read the devotional at the beginning, middle, or close of each day, anticipate nourishing your soul. Invite the Holy Spirit to guide you, to engage your heart, mind, and spirit.

Throughout your devotional time, *listen*. Each day begins with a passage to read in your own Bible, and then a devotional reading that connects story and Scripture, with topics like prayer; God's presence; the attributes of Father, Son, and Holy Spirit; and your purpose and your power when abiding in Him. After that, you have opportunity to *reflect* and *renew* with additional Bible passages and prayer points. You'll be drawn into conversation: The Word of God is active and alive, and through it, Christ can speak powerfully. Pray with the Scriptures. Ask God, What is your invitation to me through the text? And listen for His loving response.

As you close your devotional time each day, allow the truths you meditated on to sink deeply into your heart—to steady and to reassure you. Cling to Him and the truths imparted as you go about your day. Remember: God's presence goes with you. And His promise of rest remains, wherever you go, whatever your circumstance, and no matter how great your need. Most of all, take heart: the One who commands the wind and the waves also lives within you!

My soul clings to You; Your right hand takes hold of me.
Psalm 63:8 NASB

Anna Haggard
General Editor
Moments with God for Women

MOMENTS WITH GOD

for Women

1

God Hears Everything

Read 1 Kings 18:25-27, 30-38

One of the longest-recorded postal delays in history lasted eighty-nine years. In 2008, a homeowner in the United Kingdom received an invitation to a party originally mailed in 1919 to a former resident of her address. The note was placed in her mailbox via the Royal Mail, but the reason behind its long delay remains a mystery.

Even the best human efforts at communication sometimes let us down, but Scripture makes clear that God never fails to hear His faithful people. In 1 Kings 18, Elijah demonstrated the striking contrast between the pagan god Baal and Jehovah God. In a showdown to demonstrate who the true God was, after Baal's prophets had prayed for hours, Elijah taunted them: "Shout louder! . . . Surely he is a god! Perhaps he is deep in thought, or busy, or traveling. Maybe he is sleeping and must be awakened" (v. 27). Then Elijah prayed for Jehovah to answer so that His people might return to faith, and God's power was clearly displayed.

While our prayers may not always be answered as immediately as Elijah's was, we can be assured that God hears them (Psalm 34:17). The Bible reminds us that He treasures our prayers so much that He keeps them before Him in "golden bowls," like precious incense (Revelation 5:8). God will answer every prayer in His own perfect wisdom and way. There are no lost letters in heaven.

MOMENTS FOR REFLECTION

The fire of the LORD fell and burned up the sacrifice, the wood, the stones and the soil, and also licked up the water in the trench. 1 Kings 18:38

The righteous cry out, and the LORD hears them; he delivers them from all their troubles. Psalm 34:17

The LORD directs the steps of the godly. He delights in every detail of their lives. Though they stumble, they will never fall, the LORD holds them by the hand. Psalm 37:23–24 NLT

MOMENTS FOR RENEWAL

Bring to God a desire, dream, or prayer that has gone unfulfilled. Listen to His heart for you.

2

Jesus's Promise to You

Read John 14:15–21, 25–27

Jason wailed as his parents handed him over to Amy. It was the two-year-old's first time in the nursery while Mom and Dad attended the service—and he was not happy. Amy assured them he'd be fine. She tried to soothe him with toys and books, by rocking in a chair, walking around, standing still, and talking about what fun he could have. But everything was met with bigger tears and louder cries. Then she whispered five simple words in his ear: "I will stay with you." Peace and comfort quickly came.

Jesus offered His friends similar words of comfort during the week of His crucifixion: "The Father . . . will give you another advocate to help you and be with you forever—the Spirit of truth" (John 14:16–17). After His resurrection He gave them this promise: "Surely I am with you always, to the very end of the age" (Matthew 28:20). Jesus was soon to ascend to heaven, but He would send the Spirit to "stay" and live within His people.

We experience the Spirit's comfort and peace when our tears flow. We receive His guidance when we're wondering what to do (John 14:26). He opens our eyes to understand more of God (Ephesians 1:17–20), and He helps us in our weakness and prays for us (Romans 8:26–27). He stays with us forever.

In the same way, the Spirit helps us in our weakness. We do not know what we ought to pray for, but the Spirit himself intercedes for us through wordless groans. And he who searches our hearts knows the mind of the Spirit, because the Spirit intercedes for God's people in accordance with the will of God. Romans 8:26–27

But the Helper, the Holy Spirit, whom the Father will send in My name, He will teach you all things, and bring to your remembrance all things that I said to you. John 14:26 NKJV

Surely I am with you always, to the very end of the age. Matthew 28:20

MOMENTS FOR RENEWAL

How thankful I am that you remain always by my side, Jesus! I need you.

3

Depths of Love

Read 1 John 3:1-6

Three-year-old Dylan McCoy had just learned to swim when he fell through a rotted plywood covering into a forty-foot deep, stone-walled well in his grandfather's backyard. Dylan managed to stay afloat in ten feet of water until his father went down to rescue him. Firefighters brought ropes to raise the boy, but the father was so worried about his son that he'd already climbed down the slippery rocks to make sure he was safe.

Oh, the love of a parent! Oh, the lengths (and depths) we will go for our children!

When the apostle John writes to believers in the early church who were struggling to find footing for their faith as false teaching swirled about them, he extends these words like a life-preserver: "See what great love the Father has lavished on us, that we should be called children of God! And that is what we are!" (1 John 3:1). Naming believers in Jesus as "children" of God was an intimate and legal labeling that brought validity to all who trust in Him.

Oh, the lengths and depths God will go for His children!

There are actions a parent will take only for their child—like Dylan's dad descending into a well to save his son. And like the ultimate act of our heavenly Father, who sent His only Son to gather us close to His heart and restore us to life with Him (vv. 5–6).

See what great love the Father has lavished on us, that we should be called children of God! And that is what we are! 1 John 3:1

Yet to all who did receive him, to those who believed in his name, he gave the right to become children of God—children born not of natural descent, nor of human decision or a husband's will, but born of God. John 1:12–13

Yet the LORD longs to be gracious to you; therefore he will rise up to show you compassion. For the LORD is a God of justice. Blessed are all who wait for him! Isaiah 30:18

MOMENTS FOR RENEWAL

Father, thank you for reaching into the well of my need to rescue me and bring me to you!

4

The Secret
of Contentment

Read Philippians 4:10-19

When Joni Eareckson Tada returned home after suffering a swimming accident that left her a quadriplegic, her life was vastly different. Now doorways were too narrow for her wheelchair and sinks were too high. Someone had to feed her, until she decided to relearn how to feed herself. Lifting the special spoon to her mouth from her arm splint the first time, she felt humiliated as she smeared applesauce on her clothes. But she pressed on. As she says, "My secret was learning to lean on Jesus and say, 'Oh God, help me with this!'" Today she manages a spoon very well.

Joni says her confinement made her look at another captive—the apostle Paul, who was imprisoned in a Roman jail—and his letter to the Philippians. Joni strives for what Paul achieved: "I have learned to be content whatever the circumstances" (Philippians 4:11). Note that Paul had to learn to be at peace; he wasn't naturally peaceful. How did he find contentment? Through trusting in Christ: "I can do all this through him who gives me strength" (v. 13).

We all face different challenges throughout our days; and we all can look to Jesus moment by moment for help, strength, and peace. He will help us to hold back from snapping at our loved ones; He will give us the courage to do the next hard thing. Look to Him and find contentment.

MOMENTS FOR REFLECTION

> I know what it is to be in need, and I know what it is to have plenty. I have learned the secret of being content in any and every situation, whether well fed or hungry, whether living in plenty or in want. I can do all this through him who gives me strength. Philippians 4:12–13

> And my God will meet all your needs according to the riches of his glory in Christ Jesus. Philippians 4:19

MOMENTS FOR RENEWAL

Jesus, thank you for giving me courage and hope. When I feel weak, help me to find strength in you.

5

Hold Steady

Read Isaiah 41:10–13

arriet Tubman was one of the great American heroes of the nineteenth century. Showing remarkable courage, she guided more than three hundred fellow slaves to freedom after she first escaped slavery by crossing into free territory in the United States North. Not content to simply enjoy her own freedom, she ventured back into slave states nineteen times to lead friends, family, and strangers to freedom, sometimes guiding people on foot all the way to Canada.

What drove Tubman to such brave action? A woman of deep faith, she at one time said this: "I always told God, 'I'm going to hold steady on you, and you've got to see me through.'" Her dependence on God's guidance as she led people out of slavery was a hallmark of her success.

What does it mean to *hold steady* to God? A verse in the prophecy of Isaiah might help us see that in reality it's He who holds us as we grab His hand. Isaiah quotes God, who said, "I am the Lord your God who takes hold of your right hand and says to you, Do not fear; I will help you" (41:13).

Harriet held tightly to God, and He saw her through. What challenges are you facing? Hold steady to God as He "takes hold" of your hand and your life. "Do not fear." He will help you.

I am the LORD your God who takes hold of your right hand and says to you, Do not fear; I will help you. Isaiah 41:13

Fear not, for I have redeemed you; I have called you by your name; you are Mine. When you pass through the waters, I will be with you; and through the rivers, they shall not overflow you. When you walk through the fire, you shall not be burned. Isaiah 43:1–2 NKJV

The LORD is my light and my salvation—so why should I be afraid? The LORD is my fortress, protecting me from danger. Psalm 27:1 NLT

MOMENTS FOR RENEWAL

Tell God about a challenge, fear, or disappointment in your life, listening for His heart toward you as you share your circumstances with Him.

Praying like Jesus

Read Luke 22:39-44

Every coin has two sides. The front is called "heads" and, from early Roman times, usually depicts a country's head of state. The back is called "tails," a term possibly originating from the British ten pence depicting the raised tail of a heraldic lion.

Like a coin, Christ's prayer in the garden of Gethsemane possesses two sides. In the deepest hours of His life, on the night before He died on a cross, Jesus prayed, "Father, if you are willing, take this cup from me; yet not my will, but yours be done" (Luke 22:42). When Christ says, "take this cup," that's the raw honesty of prayer. He reveals His personal desire, "This is what I want."

Then Jesus turns the coin, praying "not my will." That's the side of abandon. Abandoning ourselves to God begins when we simply say, "But what do you want, God?"

This two-sided prayer is also included in Matthew 26 and Mark 14 and is mentioned in John 18. Jesus prayed both sides of prayer: take this cup (what I want, God), yet not my will (what do you want, God?), pivoting between them.

Two sides of Jesus. Two sides of prayer.

They went to a place called Gethsemane. . . . Going a little farther, [Jesus] fell to the ground and prayed that if possible the hour might pass from him. "Abba, Father," he said, "everything is possible for you. Take this cup from me. Yet not what I will, but what you will." Mark 14:32, 35–36

You will show me the path of life; in Your presence is fullness of joy; at Your right hand are pleasures forevermore. Psalm 16:11 NKJV

MOMENTS FOR RENEWAL

Father, help me follow the example of your Son, who spent everything so that I might possess real life that includes experiencing intimate prayer with you.

The Forgotten God

Read 1 Corinthians 2:6-16

When we quote The Apostles' Creed, we say, "I believe in the Holy Spirit." Author J. B. Phillips said, "Every time we say [this] we mean that we believe that [the Spirit] is a living God able and willing to enter human personality and change it."

Sometimes we forget that the Holy Spirit is not an impersonal force. The Bible describes Him as God. He possesses the attributes of God: He is present everywhere (Psalm 139:7–8), He knows all things (1 Corinthians 2:10–11), and He has infinite power (Luke 1:35). He also does things that only God can do: create (Genesis 1:2) and give life (Romans 8:2). He is equal in every way with the other Persons of the Trinity—the Father and the Son.

The Holy Spirit is a Person who engages in personal ways with us. He grieves when we sin (Ephesians 4:30). He teaches us (1 Corinthians 2:13), prays for us (Romans 8:26), guides us (John 16:13), gives us spiritual gifts (1 Corinthians 12:11), and assures us of salvation (Romans 8:16).

The Holy Spirit indwells us if we have received forgiveness of sin through Jesus. He desires to transform us so that we become more and more like Jesus. Let's cooperate with the Spirit by reading God's Word and relying on His power to obey what we learn.

The earth was formless and empty, darkness was over the surface of the deep, and the Spirit of God was hovering over the waters. Genesis 1:2

No one knows the thoughts of God except the Spirit of God. 1 Corinthian 2:11

And because you belong to him, the power of the life-giving Spirit has freed you from the power of sin that leads to death. Romans 8:2 NLT

MOMENTS FOR RENEWAL

Holy Spirit, thank you for making it possible for me to live a holy life, set apart for God. Help me to grow closer to you and to pursue the spiritual gifts you've given to me.

8

Laundry Day

Read Matthew 28:16-20

Driving through a low-income area near his church, Colorado pastor Chad Graham started praying for his "neighbors." When he noticed a small laundromat, he stopped to take a look inside and found it filled with customers. One asked Graham for a spare coin to operate the clothes dryer. That small request inspired a weekly "Laundry Day" sponsored by Graham's church. Members donate coins and soap to the laundromat, pray with customers, and support the owner of the laundry facility.

Their neighborhood outreach, which dares to include a laundromat, reflects Jesus's Great Commission to His disciples. As He said, "I have been given all authority in heaven and on earth. Go, then, to all peoples everywhere and make them my disciples: baptize them in the name of the Father, the Son, and the Holy Spirit" (Matthew 28:18–19 GNT).

His Holy Spirit's powerful presence enables everywhere outreach, including even a laundromat. Indeed, we don't go alone. As Jesus promised, "I will be with you always, to the end of the age" (v. 20 GNT).

Pastor Chad experienced that truth after praying at the laundromat for a customer named Jeff who is battling cancer. As Chad reported, "When we opened our eyes, every customer in the room was praying with us, hands stretched out toward Jeff. It was one of the most sacred moments I have experienced as a pastor."

The lesson? Let's go everywhere to proclaim Christ.

MOMENTS FOR REFLECTION

> You are the light of the world. A city that is set on a hill cannot be hidden. Matthew 5:14 NKJV

> Go, then, to all peoples everywhere and make them my disciples. Matthew 28:19 GNT

> I [Jesus] pray also for those who will believe in me through their message, that all of them may be one, Father, just as you are in me and I am in you. John 17:20–21

MOMENTS FOR RENEWAL

Ask God where He is inviting you to minister to others today or in this season, and listen for His guidance, now and throughout your day.

9

Longing for God

Read Nehemiah 1:5–11

When Conner and Sarah Smith moved five miles up the road, their cat S'mores expressed his displeasure by running away. One day Sarah saw a current photo of their old farmhouse on social media. There was S'mores in the picture!

Happily, the Smiths went to retrieve him. S'mores ran away again. Guess where he went? This time, the family that had purchased their house agreed to keep S'mores too. The Smiths couldn't stop the inevitable; S'mores would always return "home."

Nehemiah served in a prestigious position in the king's court in Susa, but his heart was elsewhere. He had just heard news of the sad condition of "the city where my ancestors are buried" (Nehemiah 2:3). And so he prayed, "Remember the instruction you gave your servant Moses, . . . 'if you return to me and obey my commands, then even if your exiled people are at the farthest horizon, I will gather them from there and bring them to the place I have chosen as a dwelling for my Name'" (1:8–9).

Home is where the heart is, they say. In Nehemiah's case, longing for home was more than being tied to the land. It was communion with God that he most desired. Jerusalem was "the place I have chosen as a dwelling for my Name."

The dissatisfaction we sense deep down is actually a longing for God. We're yearning to be home with Him.

Even if your exiled people are at the farthest horizon, I will gather them from there and bring them to the place I have chosen. Nehemiah 1:9

My Father's house has many rooms; if that were not so, would I have told you that I am going there to prepare a place for you? John 14:2

The LORD himself goes before you and will be with you; he will never leave you nor forsake you. Do not be afraid; do not be discouraged. Deuteronomy 31:8

MOMENTS FOR RENEWAL

Father, help me understand that only you can satisfy my longings. Help me be at home with you, no matter where I am.

Mighty

Read 1 Samuel 17:32, 41–47

aby Saybie, born as a "micro-preemie" at twenty-three weeks, weighed only 8.6 ounces. Doctors doubted Saybie would live and told her parents they'd likely have only an hour with their daughter. However, Saybie kept fighting. A pink card near her crib declared "Tiny but Mighty." After five months in the hospital, Saybie miraculously went home as a healthy five-pound baby. And she took a world record with her: the world's tiniest surviving baby.

It's powerful to hear stories of those who beat the odds. The Bible tells one of these stories. David, a shepherd boy, volunteered to fight Goliath—a mammoth warrior who defamed God and threatened Israel. King Saul thought David was ridiculous: "You are not able to go out against this Philistine and fight him; you are only a young man, and he has been a warrior from his youth" (1 Samuel 17:33). And when the boy David stepped onto the battlefield, Goliath "looked David over and saw that he was little more than a boy" (v. 42). However, David didn't step into battle alone. He came "in the name of the Lord Almighty, the God of the armies of Israel" (v. 45). And when the day was done, a victorious David stood above a dead Goliath.

No matter how enormous the problem, when God is with us there's nothing that we need to fear. With His strength, we're also mighty.

MOMENTS FOR REFLECTION

David said to the Philistine, "You come against me with sword and spear and javelin, but I come against you in the name of the LORD Almighty, the God of the armies of Israel, whom you have defied."
1 Samuel 17:45

What shall we say about such wonderful things as these? If God is for us, who can ever be against us?
Romans 8:31 NLT

Yes, my soul, find rest in God; my hope comes from him. Truly he is my rock and my salvation; he is my fortress, I will not be shaken. Psalm 62:5–6

MOMENTS FOR RENEWAL

Talk to God about an area of your life in which you feel small or insignificant. Tell Him you need Him, and listen for His loving response.

Before You Even Ask

Read Isaiah 65:17-25

R obert and Colleen have experienced a healthy marriage for decades. They know each other so well that one will pass the butter to the other at dinner before being asked for it. The other will refill a glass at the perfect moment. When they tell stories, they finish each other's sentences. Sometimes it seems they can read each other's mind.

It's comforting that God knows and cares for us even more than any person we know and love. When the prophet Isaiah describes the relationship between God and His people in the coming kingdom, he describes a tender, intimate relationship. God says about His people, "Before they call I will answer; while they are still speaking I will hear" (Isaiah 65:24).

But how can this be true? There are things we can pray about for years without receiving a response. As we grow in intimacy with God, aligning our hearts with His, we can begin to learn to trust in His timing and care. We can start to desire what God desires. When we pray, we ask for—among other things—the things that are part of God's kingdom as described in Isaiah 65: An end to sorrow (v. 19). Safe homes and full bellies and meaningful work for all people (vv. 21–23). Peace in the natural world (v. 25). When God's kingdom comes in its fullness, God will answer these prayers completely.

Before they call I will answer; while they are still speaking I will hear. Isaiah 65:24

"He will wipe every tear from their eyes. There will be no more death" or mourning or crying or pain, for the old order of things has passed away. . . . "I am making everything new!" Revelation 21:4–5

I am the one who answers your prayers and cares for you. I am like a tree that is always green; all your fruit comes from me. Hosea 14:8 NLT

MOMENTS FOR RENEWAL

Father, thank you for always hearing my prayers. I trust that you love me and are working all things together for good for those whom you've called. Please transform my desires so that I want what you want.

Now I See

Read John 14:15–27

Deborah Kendrick loves to attend Broadway musicals even though she is blind and always struggles to understand the setting and the movements of the characters onstage. Recently, however, she attended a play that used D-Scriptive, a new technology that conveys the visual elements of the stage production through a small FM receiver. A recorded narration, keyed to the show's light and sound boards, describes the set and the action as it unfolds onstage. Writing in *The Columbus Dispatch*, Deborah said, "If you ask me if I saw a show last week in New York, my answer is yes . . . I genuinely, unequivocally mean that I saw the show."

Her experience can serve as a vivid illustration of the Holy Spirit's role in our understanding of God's Word. Just before Jesus went to the cross, He told His followers that "the Helper, the Holy Spirit, whom the Father will send in My name, He will teach you all things, and bring to your remembrance all things that I said to you" (John 14:26 NKJV).

As we open the Bible to read or study, the Spirit of Truth is with us to guide us into all truth (16:13). On our own we are blind, but through the guidance of God's Holy Spirit we can see.

The Helper, the Holy Spirit, whom the Father will send in My name, He will teach you all things, and bring to your remembrance all things that I said to you. John 14:26 NKJV

These are the things God has revealed to us by his Spirit. The Spirit searches all things, even the deep things of God. 1 Corinthians 2:10

I pray that the eyes of your heart may be enlightened in order that you may know the hope to which he has called you, the riches of his glorious inheritance. Ephesians 1:18

MOMENTS FOR RENEWAL

Identify a word, phrase, or verse from today's Scriptures that captures your attention—and ask God about His invitation for you through the text.

13

Move Your Fence

Read Isaiah 43:18-21

The village vicar couldn't sleep. As World War II raged, he'd told a small group of American soldiers they couldn't bury their fallen comrade inside the fenced cemetery next to his church. Only burials for church members were allowed. So the men buried their beloved friend just outside the fence.

The next morning, however, the soldiers couldn't find the grave. "What happened? The grave is gone," one soldier told the reverend. "Oh, it's still there," he told him. The soldier was confused, but the churchman explained. "I regretted telling you no. So, last night, I got up—and I moved the fence."

God may give fresh perspective for our life challenges too—if we look for it. That was the prophet Isaiah's message to the downtrodden people of Israel. Instead of looking back with longing at their Red Sea rescue, they needed to shift their sight, seeing God doing new miracles, blazing new paths. "Do not dwell on the past," He urged them. "See, I am doing a new thing!" (Isaiah 43:18–19). He's our source of hope during doubts and battles. "I provide water in the wilderness and streams in the wasteland, [providing] drink to my people, my chosen [people]" (v. 20).

Refreshed with new vision, we too can see God's fresh direction in our lives. May we look with new eyes to see His new paths. Then, with courage, may we step onto new ground, bravely following Him.

See, I am doing a new thing! Now it springs up; do you not perceive it? I am making a way in the wilderness and streams in the wasteland. Isaiah 43:19

I wait for the LORD, my whole being waits, and in his word I put my hope. Psalm 130:5

O Israel, hope in the LORD; for with the LORD there is unfailing love. His redemption overflows. Psalm 130:7 NLT

MOMENTS FOR RENEWAL

Ask your heavenly Father how He wants to collaborate with you in new ways during this time—or thank Him for gifts received. Listen for His loving response.

14

Failure Is Impossible

Read Nehemiah 6:1-9

ailure is impossible!" These words were spoken by Susan B. Anthony (1820–1906), known for her immovable stance on women's rights in the US. Though she faced constant criticism and later an arrest, trial, and guilty verdict for voting illegally, Anthony vowed to never give up the fight to gain women the right to vote, believing her cause was just. Though she didn't live to see the fruit of her labor, her declaration proved true. In 1920, the nineteenth amendment to the Constitution gave women the right to vote.

Failure wasn't an option for Nehemiah either, mainly because he had a Powerful Helper: God. After asking Him to bless his cause—rebuilding the wall of Jerusalem—Nehemiah and those who had returned to Jerusalem from exile in Babylon worked to make that happen. The wall was needed to keep the people safe from enemies. But opposition to the cause came in the form of deception and threats. Nehemiah refused to let opposition deter him. He informed those who opposed the work, "I am carrying on a great project" (Nehemiah 6:3). After that, he prayed, "Now strengthen my hands" (v. 9). Thanks to perseverance, the work was completed (v. 15).

God gave Nehemiah the strength to persevere in the face of opposition. Is there a task for which you're tempted to give up? Ask God to provide whatever you need to keep going.

This work had been done with the help of our God.
Nehemiah 6:16

Blessed are those whose strength is in you, whose hearts are set on pilgrimage. As they pass through the Valley of Baka, they make it a place of springs; the autumn rains also cover it with pools. They go from strength to strength, till each appears before God.
Psalm 84:5–7

He gives power to the weak and strength to the powerless. Isaiah 40:29 NLT

MOMENTS FOR RENEWAL

Father, I need your help to keep going with the work you've given me to do, no matter what the cost may be.

Dig It Up

Read Ruth 1:3–5, 20–21

When Rebecca's brother and sister-in-law started having marriage problems, Rebecca prayed earnestly for their reconciliation. But they divorced. Then her sister-in-law took the children out of state and their dad didn't protest. Rebecca never again saw the nieces she dearly loved. Years later she said, "Because of trying to handle this sadness on my own, I let a root of bitterness start in my heart, and it began to spread to my family and friends."

The book of Ruth tells about a woman named Naomi who struggled with a heart of grief that grew into bitterness. Her husband died in a foreign land, and ten years later both her sons died. She was left destitute with her daughters-in-law, Ruth and Orpah (1:3–5). When Naomi and Ruth returned to Naomi's home country, the whole town was excited to see them. But Naomi told her friends: "The Almighty has made my life very bitter. . . . The LORD has afflicted me" (vv. 20–21). She even asked them to call her "Mara," meaning "bitter".

Who hasn't faced disappointment and been tempted toward bitterness? Someone says something hurtful, an expectation isn't met, or demands from others make us resentful. When we acknowledge to ourselves and God what's happening deep in our hearts, our tender Gardener can help us dig up any roots of bitterness—whether they're still small or have been growing for years—and can replace them with a sweet, joyful spirit.

All my longings lie open before you, Lord; my sighing is not hidden from you. Psalm 38:9

Because of the LORD's great love we are not consumed, for his compassions never fail. They are new every morning; great is your faithfulness. Lamentations 3:22–23

Get rid of all bitterness. Ephesians 4:31

MOMENTS FOR RENEWAL

Ask Jesus whether an attitude of bitterness or resentment has taken root in your heart. Place the revelation in the light of God's gentle, tender presence, listening for His heart toward you.

Right Beside You

Read Deuteronomy 4:5-8

ach day at a post office in Jerusalem, workers sort through piles of undeliverable letters in an attempt to guide each to its recipient. Many end up in a specially marked box labeled "Letters to God."

About a thousand such letters reach Jerusalem each year, addressed simply to God or Jesus. Puzzled by what to do with them, one worker began taking the letters to Jerusalem's Western Wall to have them placed between its stone blocks with other written prayers. Most of the letters ask for a job, a spouse, or good health. Some request forgiveness, others just offer thanks. One man asked God if his deceased wife could appear in his dreams because he longed to see her again. Each sender believed God would listen, if only He could be reached.

The Israelites learned much as they journeyed through the wilderness. One lesson was that their God wasn't like the other gods known at the time—distant, deaf, geographically bound, reached only by lengthy pilgrimage or international mail. No, "the LORD our God is near us whenever we pray to him" (Deuteronomy 4:7). What other people could claim that? This was revolutionary news!

God doesn't live in Jerusalem. He's close by us, wherever we are. Some still need to discover this radical truth. If only each of those letters could be sent the reply: God is right beside you. Just talk to Him.

The LORD our God is near us whenever we pray to him. Deuteronomy 4:7

He tends his flock like a shepherd: He gathers the lambs in his arms and carries them close to his heart; he gently leads those that have young. Isaiah 40:11

Can a mother forget the baby at her breast and have no compassion on the child she has borne? Though she may forget, I will not forget you! Isaiah 49:15

MOMENTS FOR RENEWAL

Father, you created the vast universe yet are closer than a breath. Thank you for being so attentive to me, listening to my every prayer.

17

The Older Brother

Read Luke 15:11–13, 17–24

Author Henri Nouwen recalls his visit to a museum in St. Petersburg, Russia, where he spent hours reflecting on Rembrandt's portrayal of the prodigal son. As the day wore on, changes in the natural lighting from a nearby window left Nouwen with the impression that he was seeing as many different paintings as there were changes of light. Each seemed to reveal something else about a father's love for his broken son.

Nouwen describes how, at about four o'clock, three figures in the painting appeared to "step forward." One was the older son who resented his father's willingness to roll out the red carpet for the homecoming of his younger brother, the prodigal. After all, hadn't he squandered so much of the family fortune, causing them pain and embarrassment in the process? (Luke 15:28–30).

The other two figures reminded Nouwen of the religious leaders who were present as Jesus told His parable. They were the ones who muttered in the background about the sinners Jesus was attracting (vv. 1–2).

Nouwen saw himself in all of them—in the wasted life of his youngest son, in the condemning older brother and religious leaders, and in a Father's heart that's big enough for anyone and everyone.

What about us? Can we see ourselves anywhere in Rembrandt's painting? In some way, every story Jesus told is about us.

But while he was still a long way off, his father saw him and was filled with compassion for him; he ran to his son, threw his arms around him and kissed him. Luke 15:20

His father said . . . "We must celebrate with a feast, for this son of mine was dead and has now returned to life. He was lost, but now he is found." So the party began. Luke 15:22–24 NLT

But [the elder son] was angry and would not go in. Therefore his father came out and pleaded with him. Luke 15:28 NKJV

MOMENTS FOR RENEWAL

Identify the character in the story of the prodigal son with whom you most identify, and talk to God about it. What is His response to you?

Talk, Trust, Feel

Read Romans 8:14–21

*D*on't talk, don't trust, don't feel was the law we lived by," says Frederick Buechner in his powerful memoir *Telling Secrets*, "and woe to the one who broke it." Buechner is describing his experience of what he calls the "unwritten law of families who for one reason or another have gone out of whack." In his own family, that "law" meant Buechner was not allowed to talk about or grieve his father's suicide, leaving him with no one he could trust with his pain.

Can you relate? In one way or another, we have often learned to live with a warped version of love, one that demands dishonesty or silence about pain or dysfunction. That kind of "love" relies on fear for control—and is a kind of slavery.

We can't afford to forget just how different Jesus's invitation to love is from the kind of conditional love we often experience—a kind of love we're always afraid we could lose. As Paul explains, through Christ's love we can finally understand what it means to not live in fear (Romans 8:15) and start to understand the kind of glorious freedom (v. 21) that's possible when we know we're deeply, truly, and unconditionally loved. We're free to talk, to trust, and to feel once more—to learn what it means to live unafraid.

MOMENTS FOR REFLECTION

Perfect love drives out fear. 1 John 4:18

"Though the mountains be shaken and the hills be removed, yet my unfailing love for you will not be shaken nor my covenant of peace be removed," says the LORD, who has compassion on you. Isaiah 54:10

The Spirit you received does not make you slaves, so that you live in fear again. Romans 8:15

MOMENTS FOR RENEWAL

Heal my heart, and help me believe in and live for the freedom your love makes possible.

19

Joyful Learning

Read Romans 12:1-3

In the city of Mysore, India, there's a school made of two refurbished train cars connected end-to-end. Local educators teamed up with the South Western Railway Company to buy and remodel the discarded coaches. The units were essentially large metal boxes, unusable until workers installed stairways, fans, lights, and desks. Workers also painted the walls and added colorful murals inside and out. Now, sixty students attend classes there because of the amazing transformation that took place.

Something even more amazing takes place when we follow the apostle Paul's command to "be transformed by the renewing of your mind" (Romans 12:2). As we allow the Holy Spirit to detach us from the world and its ways, our thoughts and attitudes begin to change. We become more loving, more hopeful, and filled with inner peace (8:6).

Something else happens too. Although this transformation process is ongoing, and often has more stops and starts than a train ride, the process helps us understand what God wants for our lives. It takes us to a place where we "will learn to know God's will" (12:2 NLT). Learning His will may or may not involve specifics, but it always involves aligning ourselves with His character and His work in the world.

Nali Kali, the name of the transformed school in India, means "joyful learning" in English. How's God's transforming power leading you to the joyful learning of His will?

MOMENTS FOR REFLECTION

> Do not conform to the pattern of this world, but be transformed by the renewing of your mind. Then you will be able to test and approve what God's will is—his good, pleasing and perfect will. Romans 12:2

> The mind governed by the flesh is death, but the mind governed by the Spirit is life and peace. Romans 8:6

> We now have this light shining in our hearts, but we ourselves are like fragile clay jars containing this great treasure. This makes it clear that our great power is from God, not from ourselves. 2 Corinthians 4:7 NLT

MOMENTS FOR RENEWAL

Father, I invite you to transform me by renewing my mind today. Thank you for all that's possible when I surrender to you.

Surprised by Grace

Read Acts 9:1–19

A woman from Grand Rapids, Michigan, fell asleep on the couch after her husband had gone to bed. An intruder sneaked in through the sliding door, which the couple had forgotten to lock, and crept through the house. He entered the bedroom where the husband was sleeping and picked up the television set. The sleeping man woke up, saw a figure standing there, and whispered, "Honey, come to bed." The burglar panicked, put down the TV, grabbed a stack of money from the dresser, and ran out.

The thief was in for a big surprise! The money turned out to be a stack of Christian pamphlets with a likeness of a twenty-dollar bill on one side and an explanation of the love and forgiveness God offers to people on the other side. Instead of the cash he expected, the intruder got the story of God's love for him.

We have to wonder what Saul expected when he realized it was Jesus appearing to him on the road to Damascus, since he had been persecuting and even killing Jesus's followers (Acts 9:1–9). Saul, later called Paul, must have been surprised by God's grace toward him, which he called "a gift": "I became a servant of this gospel by the gift of God's grace given me through the working of his power" (Ephesians 3:7).

Have you been surprised by God's gift of grace in your life as He shows you His love and forgiveness?

So Ananias went and found Saul. He laid his hands on him and said, "Brother Saul, the Lord Jesus, who appeared to you on the road, has sent me so that you might regain your sight and be filled with the Holy Spirit." Instantly something like scales fell from Saul's eyes, and he regained his sight. Acts 9:17–18 NLT

God saved you by his grace when you believed. And you can't take credit for this; it is a gift from God. Ephesians 2:8 NLT

Praise the LORD! Oh give thanks to the LORD, for He is good; for His mercy is everlasting. Psalm 106:1 NASB

MOMENTS FOR RENEWAL

Jesus, thank you for the gift of grace: a gift that cost you everything so that I might live.

21

The Privilege of Prayer

Read 1 Chronicles 29:11-19

Country artist Chris Stapleton's deeply personal song, "Daddy Doesn't Pray Anymore," was inspired by his own father's prayers for him. The poignant lyrics reveal the reason his father's prayers ended: not disillusionment or weariness, but his own death. Stapleton imagines that now, instead of speaking with Jesus in prayer, his dad is walking and talking face-to-face with Jesus.

As the prayers of Stapleton's father influenced his life, so too did a biblical father's prayer for his son. As King David's life ebbed away, he made preparations for his son Solomon to take over as the next king of Israel.

After assembling the nation together to anoint Solomon, David led the people in prayer, as he'd done many times before. As David recounted God's faithfulness to Israel, he prayed for the people to remain loyal to Him. Then he included a personal prayer specifically for his son, asking God to "give my son Solomon the wholehearted devotion to keep your commands, statutes and decrees" (1 Chronicles 29:19).

We too have the remarkable privilege to faithfully pray for the people God has placed in our lives. Our example of faithfulness can make an indelible impact that will remain even after we're gone. Just as God continued to work out the answers to David's prayers for Solomon and Israel after he was gone, so too the impact of our prayers outlives us.

MOMENTS FOR REFLECTION

> Yours, LORD, is the greatness and the power and the glory and the majesty and the splendor, for everything in heaven and earth is yours. Yours, LORD, is the kingdom; you are exalted as head over all. Wealth and honor come from you; you are the ruler of all things. In your hands are strength and power to exalt and give strength to all. Now, our God, we give you thanks, and praise your glorious name. 1 Chronicles 29:11–13

> Pray in the Spirit on all occasions with all kinds of prayers and requests. With this in mind, be alert and always keep on praying for all the Lord's people. Ephesians 6:18

> Pray without ceasing. 1 Thessalonians 5:17 NASB

MOMENTS FOR RENEWAL

Father, I bring my loved ones before you and ask that you would work out your plans in their lives.

The Craftsman's Touch

Read Exodus 31:1–5

The secret to the rich sounds of the world-famous Steinway piano? The craftsman's touch. Meticulous care goes into its creation: From the cutting of trees until the piano appears on a showroom floor, the Steinway goes through countless delicate adjustments by more than two hundred skilled craftsmen. When the yearlong process is complete, accomplished musicians play the piano and often comment on how the same vibrant tones could never be produced by an assembly line.

When the tabernacle was built, we see that God also valued the craftsman's touch. He chose the craftsman Bezalel and said of him: "I have filled him with the Spirit of God, with wisdom, with understanding, with knowledge and with all kinds of skills—to make artistic designs for work in gold, silver and bronze, to cut and set stones, to work in wood, and to engage in all kinds of crafts" (Exodus 31:3–5).

Today God dwells in the hearts of believers. Yet the call to craftsmanship has not ended. Now each individual believer is God's "masterpiece" (Ephesians 2:10 NLT). The Master Craftsman is the Holy Spirit, who chips away at flaws in our character to make each of us like Jesus (Romans 8:28–29). And as we yield to His workmanship, we will find that the secret to the final product is the Craftsman's touch.

I have filled [Bezalel] with the Spirit of God, with wisdom, with understanding, with knowledge and with all kinds of skills—to make artistic designs for work in gold, silver and bronze, to cut and set stones, to work in wood, and to engage in all kinds of crafts. Exodus 31:3–5

We are God's masterpiece. He has created us anew in Christ Jesus, so we can do the good things he planned for us long ago. Ephesians 2:10 NLT

For you created my inmost being; you knit me together in my mother's womb. I praise you because I am fearfully and wonderfully made. Psalm 139:13–14

MOMENTS FOR RENEWAL

Ask the Holy Spirit what aspects of God's personality, character, and nature He's uniquely inlaid in you, while praising Him for your being "fearfully and wonderfully made."

23

Carried through the Storm

Read Psalm 107:1-3, 23-32

During Scottish missionary Alexander Duff's first voyage to India in 1830, he was shipwrecked in a storm off the coast of South Africa. He and his fellow passengers made it to a small, desolate island; and a short time later, one of the crew found a copy of a Bible belonging to Duff washed ashore on the beach. When the book dried, Duff read Psalm 107 to his fellow survivors, and they took courage. Finally, after a rescue and yet another shipwreck, Duff arrived in India.

Psalm 107 lists some of the ways God delivered the Israelites. Duff and his shipmates no doubt identified with and took comfort in the words: "He stilled the storm to a whisper; the waves of the sea were hushed. They were glad when it grew calm, and he guided them to their desired haven" (vv. 29–30). And, like the Israelites, they too "[gave] thanks to the LORD for his unfailing love and his wonderful deeds for mankind" (v. 31).

We see a parallel to Psalm 107:28–30 in the New Testament (Matthew 8:23–27; Mark 4:35–41). Jesus and His disciples were in a boat at sea when a violent storm began. His disciples cried out in fear, and Jesus—God in flesh—calmed the sea. We too can take courage! Our powerful God and Savior hears and responds to our cries and comforts us in the midst of our storms.

MOMENTS FOR REFLECTION

> He stilled the storm to a whisper; the waves of the sea were hushed. Psalm 107:29

> A furious squall came up, and the waves broke over the boat, so that it was nearly swamped. . . . [Jesus] got up, rebuked the wind and said to the waves, "Quiet! Be still!" Then the wind died down and it was completely calm. Mark 4:37, 39

> Be still, and know that I am God. Psalm 46:10 NKJV

MOMENTS FOR RENEWAL

Father, thank you for not leaving me to face the storms on my own. I need you!

24

Our Compassionate God

Read Psalm 138

The winter night was cold when someone threw a large stone through a Jewish child's bedroom window. A star of David had been displayed in the window, along with a menorah to celebrate Hanukkah, the Jewish Festival of Lights. In the child's town of Billings, Montana, thousands of people—many of them believers in Jesus— responded to the hateful act with compassion. Choosing to identify with the hurt and fear of their Jewish neighbors, they pasted pictures of menorahs in their own windows.

As believers in Jesus, we too receive great compassion. Our Savior humbled himself to live among us (John 1:14), identifying with us. On our behalf, He, "being in very nature God . . . made himself nothing by taking the very nature of a servant" (Philippians 2:6–7). Then, feeling as we feel and weeping as we weep, He died on a cross, sacrificing His life to save ours.

Nothing we struggle with is beyond our Savior's concern. If someone "throws rocks" at our lives, He comforts us. If life brings disappointments, He walks with us through despair. "Though the LORD is exalted, he looks kindly on the lowly; though lofty, he sees them from afar" (Psalm 138:6). In our troubles, He preserves us, stretching out His hand against both "the anger of [our] foes" (v. 7) and our own deepest fears. Thank you, God, for your compassionate love.

Though the LORD is exalted, he looks kindly on the lowly; though lofty, he sees them from afar. Psalm 138:6

The Word became human and made his home among us. He was full of unfailing love and faithfulness. And we have seen his glory, the glory of the Father's one and only Son. John 1:14 NLT

[Jesus], being in very nature God, did not consider equality with God something to be used to his own advantage; rather, he made himself nothing by taking the very nature of a servant, being made in human likeness. Philippians 2:6–7

MOMENTS FOR RENEWAL

Father, thank you for your compassionate, unchanging love and for your nearness when I'm alone, disillusioned, or afraid.

Divine Rescue

Read Exodus 3:7-10

After being informed of a 911 call from a concerned citizen, a police officer drove alongside the train tracks, shining his floodlight into the dark until he spotted the vehicle straddling the iron rails. The trooper's dashboard camera captured the harrowing scene as a train barreled toward the car. "That train was coming fast," the officer said, "Fifty to eighty miles per hour." Acting without hesitation, he pulled an unconscious man from the car mere seconds before the train slammed into it.

Scripture reveals God as the One who rescues—often precisely when all seems lost. Trapped in Egypt and withering under suffocating oppression, the Israelites imagined no possibility for escape. In Exodus, however, we find God offering them words resounding with hope: "I have indeed seen the misery of my people in Egypt," He said. "I have heard them crying out . . . and I am concerned about their suffering" (3:7). And God not only saw—God acted. "I have come down to rescue them" (v. 8). God led Israel out of bondage. This was a divine rescue.

God's rescue of Israel reveals God's heart—and His power—to help all of us who are in need. He assists those of us who are destined for ruin unless God arrives to save us. Though our situation may be dire or impossible, we can lift our eyes and heart and watch for the One who loves to rescue.

Now the length of time the Israelite people lived in Egypt was 430 years. Exodus 12:40

The LORD said, "I have indeed seen the misery of my people in Egypt. I have heard them crying out because of their slave drivers, and I am concerned about their suffering. So I have come down to rescue them." Exodus 3:7–8

The LORD will fight for you; you need only to be still. Exodus 14:14

MOMENTS FOR RENEWAL

Bring to God a situation, whether in your life or in someone else's, that is so desperate it appears hopeless. Cry out for His Help. How does He respond?

26

Plans Disrupted

Read Acts 16:6–10

Jane's plans to become a speech therapist ended when an internship revealed the job was too emotionally challenging for her. Then she was given the opportunity to write for a magazine. She'd never seen herself as an author, but years later she found herself advocating for needy families through her writing. "Looking back, I can see why God changed my plans," she says. "He had a bigger plan for me."

The Bible has many stories of disrupted plans. On his second missionary journey, Paul had sought to bring the gospel into Bithynia, but the Spirit of Jesus stopped him (Acts 16:6–7). This must have seemed mystifying: why was Jesus disrupting plans that were in line with a God-given mission? The answer came in a dream one night: Macedonia needed him even more. There, Paul would plant the first church in Europe. Solomon also observed, "Many are the plans in a person's heart, but it is the LORD's purpose that prevails" (Proverbs 19:21).

It's sensible to make plans. A well-known adage goes, "Fail to plan, and you plan to fail." But God may disrupt our plans with His own. Our challenge is to listen and obey, knowing we can trust God. If we submit to His will, we'll find ourselves fitting into His purpose for our lives.

As we continue to make plans, we can add a new twist: Plan to listen. Listen to God's plan.

MOMENTS FOR REFLECTION

You can make many plans, but the LORD's purpose will prevail. Proverbs 19:21 NLT

The Holy Spirit had prevented them from preaching the word in the province of Asia at that time. Then coming to the borders of Mysia, they headed north for the province of Bithynia, but again the Spirit of Jesus did not allow them to go there. Acts 16:6–7 NLT

I will instruct you and teach you in the way you should go. Psalm 32:8

MOMENTS FOR RENEWAL

Father, give me the faith to listen to you when my plans are disrupted, knowing that you have a greater purpose for my life.

Insight from the Spirit

Read John 16:12-15

As the French soldier dug in the desert sand, reinforcing the defenses of his army's encampment, he had no idea he would make a momentous discovery. Moving another shovelful of sand, he saw a stone. Not just any stone. It was the Rosetta Stone, containing laws and governance from King Ptolemy V written in three languages. That stone (now housed in the British Museum) would be one of the most important archaeological finds of the nineteenth century, helping to unlock the mysteries of the ancient Egyptian writing known as hieroglyphics.

Much of Scripture is also wrapped in deep mystery. Still, the night before the cross, Jesus promised His followers that He would send the Holy Spirit. He told them, "But when he, the Spirit of truth, comes, he will guide you into all the truth. He will not speak on his own; he will speak only what he hears, and he will tell you what is yet to come" (John 16:13). The Holy Spirit is, in a sense, our divine Rosetta Stone, shedding light on the truth—including truths behind the mysteries of the Bible.

While we're not promised absolute understanding of everything in the Scriptures, we can have confidence that by the Spirit we can comprehend everything necessary to follow Jesus. He will guide us into those vital truths.

When he, the Spirit of truth, comes, he will guide you into all the truth. John 16:13

For the word of God is living and powerful, and sharper than any two-edged sword, piercing even to the division of soul and spirit, and of joints and marrow, and is a discerner of the thoughts and intents of the heart. Hebrews 4:12 NKJV

Teach me Your way, O LORD; I will walk in Your truth; unite my heart to fear Your name. Psalm 86:11 NKJV

MOMENTS FOR RENEWAL

Talk to God about a Bible passage that troubles or puzzles you, and ask the Holy Spirit to guide you into a better understanding of it.

28

Abundant Waters

Read Exodus 17:1-7

In Australia, a report outlined "a grim story" of extreme drought, heat, and fire. The account described a horrific year with only minuscule rainfall, turning parched brush into tinder. Raging fires torched the countryside. Fish died. Crops failed. All because they didn't have a simple resource we often take for granted—water, which we all need in order to live.

Israel found itself in its own terrifying dilemma. As the people camped in the dusty, barren desert, we read this alarming line: "There was no water for the people to drink" (Exodus 17:1). The people were afraid. Their throats were dry. The sand sizzled. Their children suffered thirst. Terrified, the people "quarreled with Moses," demanding water (v. 2). But what could Moses do? He could only go to God.

And God gave Moses odd instructions: "Take . . . the staff [and] . . . strike the rock, and water will come out of it for the people to drink" (vv. 5–6). So Moses hit the rock, and out gushed a river, plenty for the people and their cattle. That day, Israel knew that their God loved them. Their God provided abundant water.

If you're experiencing a drought or wilderness in life, know that God is aware of it and He's with you. Whatever your need, whatever your lack, may you find hope and refreshment in His abundant waters.

As the deer pants for streams of water, so my soul pants for you, my God. My soul thirsts for God, for the living God. When can I go and meet with God? Psalm 42:1–2

He opened the rock, and water gushed out; it flowed like a river in the desert. Psalm 105:41

My soul thirsts for You; my flesh longs for You in a dry and thirsty land where there is no water. Psalm 63:1 NKJV

MOMENTS FOR RENEWAL

If you are in a wilderness season, talk to God about it, honestly expressing how you feel. Listen for His heart toward you.

29

Knowing the Father

Read John 14:8–11

According to legend, British conductor Sir Thomas Beecham once saw a distinguished-looking woman in a hotel foyer. Believing he knew her but unable to remember her name, he paused to talk with her. As the two chatted, he vaguely recollected that she had a brother. Hoping for a clue, he asked how her brother was doing and whether he was still working at the same job. "Oh, he's very well," she said, "And still king."

A case of mistaken identity can be embarrassing, as it was for Sir Beecham. But at other times it may be more serious, as it was for Jesus's disciple Philip. The disciple knew Christ, of course, but he hadn't fully appreciated who He was. He wanted Jesus to "show [them] the Father," and Jesus responded, "Anyone who has seen me has seen the Father" (John 14:8–9). As God's unique Son, Christ reveals the Father so perfectly that to know one is to know the other (vv. 10–11).

If we ever wonder what God is like in His character, personality, or concern for others, we only need to look to Jesus to find out. Christ's character, kindness, love, and mercy reveal God's character. And although our amazing, awesome God is beyond our complete comprehension and understanding, we have a tremendous gift in what He's revealed of Himself in Jesus.

Jesus answered: "Don't you know me, Philip, even after I have been among you such a long time? Anyone who has seen me has seen the Father." John 14:9

The Son is the image of the invisible God, the first-born over all creation. For in him all things were created: things in heaven and on earth, visible and invisible, whether thrones or powers or rulers or authorities; all things have been created through him and for him. Colossians 1:15–16

Now to the King eternal, immortal, invisible, the only God, be honor and glory for ever and ever. 1 Timothy 1:17

MOMENTS FOR RENEWAL

Father, thank you for revealing who you are—your personality, your character, and your boundless love—through your Son, Jesus.

30

The Discipline of Waiting

Read Psalm 40:1-3

Waiting is hard. We wait in grocery lines, in traffic, in the doctor's office. We twiddle our thumbs, stifle our yawns, and fret inwardly in frustration. On another level, we wait for a letter that doesn't come, for a prodigal child to return, or for a spouse to change. We wait for a child we can hold in our arms. We wait for our heart's desire.

In Psalm 40, David says, "I waited patiently for the LORD" (v. 1). The original language here suggests that David "waited and waited and waited" for God to answer his prayer. Yet as he looks back at this time of delay, he praises God. As a result, David says, God "put a new song . . . a hymn of praise" in his heart (40:3).

"What a chapter can be written of God's delays!" said F. B. Meyer. "It is the mystery of educating human spirits to the finest temper of which they are capable." Through the discipline of waiting, we can develop the quieter virtues—humility, patience, joyful endurance, persistence—virtues that take the longest to learn.

What do we do when God seems to withhold our heart's desire? He is able to help us to love and trust Him enough to accept the delay with joy and to see it as an opportunity to develop character—and to praise Him.

I waited patiently for the LORD; he turned to me and heard my cry. Psalm 40:1

Endurance develops strength of character, and character strengthens our confident hope of salvation. And this hope will not lead to disappointment. For we know how dearly God loves us, because he has given us the Holy Spirit to fill our hearts with his love. Romans 5:4–5 NLT

I remain confident of this: I will see the goodness of the LORD in the land of the living. Wait for the LORD; be strong and take heart and wait for the LORD. Psalm 27:13–14

MOMENTS FOR RENEWAL

If you're waiting on God to act, honestly express how you feel about your circumstances with God. Listen for His loving response.

31

Pleading with God

Read Daniel 9:1–5, 17–19

A family's prayer time ended with a surprising announcement one morning. As soon as Dad said, "Amen," five-year-old Kaitlyn proclaimed, "And I prayed for Logan, because he had his eyes open during prayer."

Praying for your ten-year-old brother's prayer protocol likely isn't what Scripture has in mind when it calls us to intercessory prayer, but at least Kaitlyn realized that we can pray for others.

Bible teacher Oswald Chambers emphasized the importance of praying for someone else. He said that "intercession is putting yourself in God's place; it is having His mind and perspective." It's praying for others in light of what we know about God and His love for us.

We find a great example of intercessory prayer in Daniel 9. The prophet understood God's troubling promise that the Jews would have seventy years of captivity in Babylon (Jeremiah 25:11–12; 29:10). Realizing that those years were nearing their completion, Daniel went into prayer mode. He referenced God's commands (Daniel 9:4–6), humbled himself (v. 8), honored His character (v. 9), confessed sin (v. 15), and depended on His mercy as he prayed for His people (v. 18). And he got an immediate answer from God (v. 21).

Not all prayer ends with such a dramatic response, but be encouraged that we can go to God on behalf of others with an attitude of trust and dependence on Him.

This is what the LORD says: "When seventy years are completed for Babylon, I will come to you and fulfill my good promise to bring you back to this place."

Jeremiah 29:10

I, Daniel, understood from the Scriptures. . . . So I turned to the Lord God and pleaded with him in prayer and petition, in fasting, and in sackcloth and ashes. Daniel 9:2–3

While I was still in prayer, Gabriel, the man I had seen in the earlier vision, came to me in swift flight. Daniel 9:21

MOMENTS FOR RENEWAL

Father, have mercy on me and those I love, and lead us in ways that are just, holy, and pleasing to you.

32

Awake to the Holy Spirit

Read Luke 1:35–41

Of the three Persons of the Trinity, the Holy Spirit is often the least understood or discussed, perhaps partly because of the humble, behind-the-scenes role He plays in orchestrating God's plans and purposes in our lives.

That's why we are being alerted to pay attention to the workings of the often "forgotten God" when Luke mentions the Holy Spirit seven times in the first two chapters of his gospel. The Holy Spirit is active in the lives of the unborn John the Baptist (1:15), Mary (1:35), Elizabeth (1:41), Zacharias (1:67), and Simeon (2:25–27). Here, in what we often call "the Christmas story," the Holy Spirit is identified as the One who guided Simeon, filled Zacharias and Elizabeth, and created the baby in Mary's womb.

Do we, like them, recognize the Spirit's voice in the midst of all others? Are we attentive to His promptings and ready to listen to Him and His ways? Will we allow His warmth and love to fill our hearts and flow through our hands? Today, may we be awake to the One who is alive and active: the true, eternal Spirit of Christ within us.

He [John the Baptist] will also be filled with the Holy
Spirit, even from his mother's womb. Luke 1:15 NKJV

The Holy Spirit will come upon you [Mary], and
the power of the Highest will overshadow you.
Luke 1:35 NKJV

When Elizabeth heard Mary's greeting, the baby
leaped in her womb, and Elizabeth was filled with
the Holy Spirit. Luke 1:41

MOMENTS FOR RENEWAL

*Father, awaken me more and more to the leading and guiding of the
Spirit of Christ alive and active in me.*

33

Hotel Corona

Read 2 Corinthians 5:14–20

The Dan Hotel in Jerusalem became known by a different name in 2020—"Hotel Corona." The government dedicated the hotel to patients recovering from COVID-19, and the hotel became known as a rare site of joy and unity during a difficult time. Since the residents already had the virus, they were free to sing, dance, and laugh together. And they did! In a country where tensions between different political and religious groups run high, the shared crisis created a space where people could learn to see each other as human beings first—and even become friends.

It's natural, normal even, for us to be drawn toward those we see as similar to us, people we suspect share similar experiences and values to our own. But as the apostle Paul often emphasized, the gospel is a challenge to any barriers between human beings that we see as "normal" (2 Corinthians 5:15). Through the lens of the gospel, we see a bigger picture than our differences—a shared brokenness and a shared longing and need to experience healing in God's love.

If we believe that "one died for all," then we can also no longer be content with surface-level assumptions about others. Instead, "Christ's love compels us" (v. 14) to share His love and mission with those God loves more than we can imagine—all of us.

Christ's love compels us, because we are convinced that one died for all. . . . From now on we regard no one from a worldly point of view. 2 Corinthians 5:14, 16

All are justified freely by his grace. Romans 3:24

In this new life, it doesn't matter if you are a Jew or a Gentile, circumcised or uncircumcised, barbaric, uncivilized, slave, or free. Christ is all that matters, and he lives in all of us. Colossians 3:11 NLT

MOMENTS FOR RENEWAL

Father, thank you for those moments when I see a glimmer of breathtaking beauty through the love and joy of others. Help me to live each day this way, regarding "no one from a worldly point of view."

34

Sinking into Grace

Read Psalm 127

Finally, on January 8, 1964, seventeen-year-old Randy Gardner did something he hadn't done for eleven days and twenty-five minutes: he nodded off to sleep. He wanted to beat The Guinness Book of Records (today known as the *Guinness World Records*) for how long a human could stay awake. By drinking soft drinks and hitting the basketball court and bowling alley, Gardner rebuffed sleep for a week and a half. Before finally collapsing, his sense of taste, smell, and hearing went haywire. Decades later, Gardner suffered from severe bouts of insomnia. He set the record but also confirmed the obvious: sleep is essential.

Many of us struggle to get a decent night's rest. Unlike Gardner who deprived himself intentionally, we might suffer sleeplessness for a number of reasons—including a mountain of anxieties: the fear of all we need to accomplish, the dread of others' expectations, the distress of living at a frantic pace. Sometimes it's hard for us to turn off the fear and relax.

The psalmist tells us that "unless the LORD builds the house," we labor in vain (Psalm 127:1). Our "toiling" and our relentless efforts are useless unless God provides what we need. Thankfully, God does provide what we need. He "grants sleep to those he loves" (v. 2). And God's love extends to all of us. He invites us to release our anxieties to Him and sink into His rest, into His grace.

Unless the LORD builds the house, the builders labor in vain. . . . In vain you rise early and stay up late, toiling for food to eat—for he grants sleep to those he loves. Psalm 127:1–2

Cast all your anxiety on him because he cares for you. 1 Peter 5:7

He will not let you stumble; the one who watches over you will not slumber. Indeed, he who watches over Israel never slumbers or sleeps. Psalm 121:3–4 NLT

MOMENTS FOR RENEWAL

Ask God to grant you a good night's sleep tonight—and the remembrance that He empowers and enables you to do your work today.

35

The Will of God

Read Psalm 62

God's will is sometimes hard to follow. He asks us to do the right things. He calls us to endure hardship without complaining; to love awkward people; to heed the voice inside us that says, You mustn't; to take steps we'd rather not take. So, we must tell our souls all day long: "Hey soul, listen up. Be silent: Do what Jesus is asking you to do."

"My soul waits in silence for God alone" (Psalm 62:1 NASB). "My soul, wait in silence for God alone" (62:5 NASB). The verses are similar, but different. David says something about his soul; then says something to his soul. "Waits in silence" addresses a decision, a settled state of mind. "Wait in silence" is David stirring his soul to remember that decision.

David determines to live in silence—quiet submission to God's will. This is our calling as well, the thing for which we were created. We'll be at peace when we've agreed: "Not my will, but yours be done" (Luke 22:42). This is our first and highest calling when we make Him Lord and the source of our deepest pleasure. "I desire to do your will," the psalmist said (Psalm 40:8).

We must always ask for God's help, of course, for our "hope comes from him" (62:5). When we ask for His help, He delivers it. God never asks us to do anything He won't or can't do.

My soul waits in silence for God alone; from Him comes my salvation. He alone is my rock and my salvation, my stronghold; I will not be greatly shaken.
Psalm 62:1–2 NASB

I take joy in doing your will, my God, for your instructions are written on my heart. Psalm 40:8 NLT

If any of you wants to be my follower, you must give up your own way, take up your cross, and follow me.
Matthew 16:24 NLT

MOMENTS FOR RENEWAL

Father, I may not always understand your will, but I ask for help to surrender to it. Teach me to trust your good and faithful character.

36

Seeking God's Help

Read 2 Chronicles 20:5–12, 15

For five years in the late 1800s, grasshoppers descended on Minnesota, destroying the crops. Farmers tried trapping the grasshoppers in tar and burning their fields to kill the eggs. Feeling desperate, and on the brink of starvation, many people sought a statewide day of prayer, yearning to seek God's help together. The governor relented, setting aside April 26 to pray.

In the days after the collective prayer, the weather warmed and the eggs started to come to life. But then four days later a drop in temperature surprised and delighted many, for the freezing temperatures killed the larvae. Minnesotans once again would harvest their crops of corn, wheat, and oats.

Prayer was also behind the saving of God's people during the reign of King Jehoshaphat. When the king learned that a vast army was coming against him, he called God's people to pray and fast. The people reminded God how He'd saved them in times past. And Jehoshaphat said that if calamity came upon them, "whether the sword of judgment, or plague or famine," they would cry out to God knowing that He would hear and save them (2 Chronicles 20:9).

God rescued His people from the invading armies, and He hears us when we cry out to Him in distress. Whatever your concern—whether a relationship issue or something threatening from the natural world—lift it to God in prayer. Nothing is too hard for Him.

This is what the LORD says: Do not be afraid! Don't be discouraged by this mighty army, for the battle is not yours, but God's. 2 Chronicles 20:15 NLT

Let us therefore come boldly to the throne of grace, that we may obtain mercy and find grace to help in time of need. Hebrews 4:16 NKJV

He reached down from on high and took hold of me; he drew me out of deep waters. Psalm 18:16

MOMENTS FOR RENEWAL

Father, you made the world and all that's in it. Please restore order and save your people, whom you love.

37

The Link to Life

Read Titus 3:1–11

By the time he was sixteen, Morris Frank (1908–1980) had lost his sight in both eyes. Several years later, he traveled to Switzerland where he met Buddy, the canine who would help to inspire Frank's involvement with the Seeing Eye guide-dog school.

With Buddy leading the way, Frank learned to navigate busy sidewalks and intersections. Describing the freedom his guide provided, Frank said, "It was glorious: just [Buddy] and a leather strap, linking me to life." Buddy gave Morris Frank a new kind of access to the world around him.

God's Holy Spirit gives us access to abundant spiritual life in Christ. When we accept Christ as Lord, God washes our sins away and renews us "by the Holy Spirit, whom he poured out on us generously through Jesus Christ our Savior" (Titus 3:5–6). Once we know Christ, the Holy Spirit helps us experience God's love (Romans 5:5), understand God's Word (John 14:26), pray (Romans 8:26), and abound in hope (Romans 15:13).

Today, as you think about your relationship with God, remember that the Spirit is your guide to life in Christ (Romans 8:14).

MOMENTS FOR REFLECTION

He saved us, not because of the righteous things we had done, but because of his mercy. He washed away our sins, giving us a new birth and new life through the Holy Spirit. Titus 3:5 NLT

Hope does not put us to shame, because God's love has been poured out into our hearts through the Holy Spirit, who has been given to us. Romans 5:5

Those who are led by the Spirit of God are the children of God. Romans 8:14

MOMENTS FOR RENEWAL

Jesus, I praise you for sending us the Holy Spirit so that I may be able to live wholeheartedly for you.

38

Accepted and Approved

Read Isaiah 43:1–4

As a child, Tenny felt insecure. He sought approval from his father, but he never received it. It seemed that whatever he did, whether in school or at home, it was never good enough. Even when he entered adulthood, the insecurity remained. He continually wondered, Am I good enough?

Only when Tenny received Jesus as his Savior did he find the security and approval he'd long yearned for. He learned that God—having created him—loved and cherished him as His son. Tenny finally could live with the confidence that he was truly valued and appreciated.

In Isaiah 43:1–4, God told His chosen people that, having formed them, He would use His power and love to redeem them. "You are precious and honored in my sight," He proclaimed. He would act on their behalf because He loved them (v. 4).

The value God places on those He loves doesn't come from anything we do, but from the simple and powerful truth that He's chosen us to be His own.

These words in Isaiah 43 not only gave Tenny great security, but also empowered him with the confidence to do his best for God in whatever task he was called to do. Today he's a pastor who does all he can to encourage others with this life-giving truth: we're accepted and approved in Jesus. May we confidently live out this truth today.

MOMENTS FOR REFLECTION

You are precious and honored in my sight . . . I love you. Isaiah 43:4

He will quiet you with His love, He will rejoice over you with singing. Zephaniah 3:17 NKJV

For he chose us in him before the creation of the world to be holy and blameless in his sight. In love he predestined us for adoption to sonship through Jesus Christ, in accordance with his pleasure and will. Ephesians 1:4–5

MOMENTS FOR RENEWAL

Imagine Jesus is lovingly gazing at you, and you at Him. Ask your Savior how He sees you.

39

Mighty Warrior

Read Judges 6:11–16

Diet Eman was an ordinary, shy young woman in the Netherlands—in love, working, and enjoying time with family and friends—when the Germans invaded in 1940. As Diet (pronounced Deet) later wrote, "When there is danger on your doorstep, you want to act almost like an ostrich burying its head in the sand." Yet Diet felt God calling her to resist the German oppressors, which included risking her life to find hiding places for Jews and other pursued people. This unassuming young woman became a warrior for God.

We find many stories in the Bible similar to Diet's, stories of God using seemingly unlikely characters to serve Him. For instance, when the angel of the Lord approached Gideon, he proclaimed, "The Lord is with you, mighty warrior" (Judges 6:12). Yet Gideon seemed anything but mighty. He'd been secretly threshing wheat away from the prying eyes of the Midianites, who oppressively controlled Israel at the time (vv. 1–6, 11). He was from the weakest clan of Israel (Manasseh) and the "least" in his family (v. 15). He didn't feel up to God's calling and even requested several signs. Yet God used him to defeat the cruel Midianites (see chapter 7).

God saw Gideon as *mighty*. And just as God was with and equipped Gideon, so God is with us, His "dearly loved children" (Ephesians 5:1)—supplying all we need to live for and serve Him in little and big ways.

MOMENTS FOR REFLECTION

The LORD is with you, mighty warrior. Judges 6:12

The Spirit of God, who raised Jesus from the dead, lives in you. And just as God raised Christ Jesus from the dead, he will give life to your mortal bodies by this same Spirit living within you. Romans 8:11 NLT

For by You I can run at a troop of warriors; and by my God I can leap over a wall. Psalm 18:29 NASB

MOMENTS FOR RENEWAL

Father, thank you for supplying me with all that I need to live for and serve you—for equipping me with your great power and strength.

40

Fluff and Other Stuff

Read Exodus 6:1-9

Winnie the Pooh famously said, "If the person you are talking to doesn't appear to be listening, be patient. It may simply be that he has a small piece of fluff in his ear."

Winnie might be on to something. When someone won't listen to you even though following your counsel would be to their advantage, it may be that their reticence is nothing more than a small piece of fluff in their ear. Or there may be another hindrance: Some folks find it hard to listen well because they're broken and discouraged.

Moses said he spoke to the people of Israel but they didn't listen because their spirits were broken and their lives were hard (Exodus 6:9). The word discouragement in the Hebrew text is literally "short of breath," the result of their bitter enslavement in Egypt. That being the case, Israel's reluctance to listen to Moses's instruction called for understanding and compassion, not censure.

What should we do when others won't listen? Winnie the Pooh's words enshrine wisdom: "Be patient." God says, "Love is patient, love is kind" (1 Corinthians 13:4); it's willing to wait. He's not finished with that individual. He's working through their sorrow, our love, and our prayers. Perhaps, in His time, He'll open their ears to hear. Just be patient.

They did not listen to him because of their discouragement and harsh labor. Exodus 6:9

Love is patient and kind. Love is not jealous or boastful or proud or rude. It does not demand its own way. It is not irritable, and it keeps no record of being wronged. It does not rejoice about injustice but rejoices whenever the truth wins out. Love never gives up, never loses faith, is always hopeful, and endures through every circumstance. 1 Corinthians 13:4–7 NLT

The faithful love of the LORD never ends! His mercies never cease. Great is his faithfulness.
Lamentations 3:22–23 NLT

MOMENTS FOR RENEWAL

Father, give me patience with those who are struggling, frustrated, or discouraged. Help me not to judge them, but to love them.

41

More Than Wishing

Read Matthew 6:5–15

As a child, C. S. Lewis enjoyed reading the books of E. Nesbit, especially *Five Children and It*. In this book, brothers and sisters on a summer holiday discover an ancient sand fairy who grants them one wish each day. But every wish brings the children more trouble than happiness because they can't foresee the results of getting everything they ask for.

The Bible tells us to make our requests known to God (Philippians 4:6). But prayer is much more than telling God what we want Him to do for us. When Jesus taught His disciples how to pray, He began by reminding them, "Your Father knows what you need before you ask him" (Matthew 6:8).

What we call "The Lord's Prayer" is more about living in a growing, trusting relationship with our heavenly Father than about getting what we want from Him. As we grow in faith, our prayers will become less of a wish list and more of an intimate conversation with the Lord.

Toward the end of his life, C. S. Lewis wrote, "If God had granted all the silly prayers I've made in my life, where should I be now?"

Prayer is placing ourselves in the presence of God to receive from Him what we really need.

Your kingdom come, your will be done, on earth as it is in heaven. Matthew 6:10

Do not be anxious about anything, but in every situation, by prayer and petition, with thanksgiving, present your requests to God. And the peace of God, which transcends all understanding, will guard your hearts and your minds in Christ Jesus. Philippians 4:6–7

Your Father knows exactly what you need even before you ask him! Matthew 6:8 NLT

MOMENTS FOR RENEWAL

Tell God what you need, thanking your Savior for His faithfulness to you throughout your life. Listen for His response to—and His heart toward—you.

42

A Remote Location

Read Mark 8:1–13

Tristan da Cunha Island is famous for its isolation. It is the most remote inhabited island in the world, thanks to the 288 people who call it home. The island is located in the South Atlantic Ocean, 1,750 miles from South Africa—the nearest mainland. Anyone who might want to drop by for a visit has to travel by boat for seven days because the island has no airstrip.

Jesus and His followers were in a somewhat remote area when He produced a miraculous meal for thousands of hungry people. Before His miracle, Jesus said to His disciples, "[These people] have already been with me three days and have nothing to eat. If I send them home hungry, they will collapse on the way" (Mark 8:2–3). Because they were in the countryside where food was not readily available, they had to depend fully on Jesus. They had nowhere else to turn.

Sometimes God allows us to end up in desolate places where He is our only source of help. His ability to provide for us is not necessarily linked with our circumstances. If He created the entire world out of nothing, God can certainly meet our needs—whatever our circumstances—out of the riches of His glory, in Christ Jesus (Philippians 4:19).

MOMENTS FOR REFLECTION

> O God, you are my God; I earnestly search for you. My soul thirsts for you; my whole body longs for you in this parched and weary land where there is no water. I have seen you in your sanctuary and gazed upon your power and glory. Psalm 63:1–2 NLT

> My God will meet all your needs according to the riches of his glory in Christ Jesus. Philippians 4:19

MOMENTS FOR RENEWAL

Tell God where you struggle to believe that He will meet your needs. Listen for His loving response to you.

43

God's Restoring Ways

Read Hosea 14

One of the most moving songs in the musical *The Greatest Showman* is "From Now On." Sung after the main character comes to some painful self-realizations about the ways he's wounded family and friends, the song celebrates the joy of coming back home and finding that what we already have is more than enough.

The book of Hosea concludes with a similar tone—one of breathless joy and gratitude at the restoration God makes possible for those who return to Him. Much of the book, which compares the relationship between God and His people to a relationship with an unfaithful spouse, grieves Israel's failures to love Him and live for Him.

But in chapter 14, Hosea lifts up the promise of God's boundless love, grace, and restoration—freely available to those who return to Him heartbroken over the ways they've abandoned Him (vv. 1–3). "I will heal their waywardness," God promises, "and love them freely" (v. 4). And what had seemed broken beyond repair will once more find wholeness and abundance, as God's grace, like dew, causes His people to "blossom like a lily" and "flourish like the grain" (vv. 5–7).

When we've hurt others or taken for granted God's goodness in our life, it's easy to assume we've forever marred the good gifts we've been given. But when we humbly turn to Him, we find His love is always reaching to embrace and restore.

People will dwell again in his shade; they will flourish like the grain, they will blossom like the vine. Hosea 14:7

I will heal you of your faithlessness; my love will know no bounds. Hosea 14:4 NLT

If God is for us, who can be against us? He who did not spare his own Son, but gave him up for us all—how will he not also, along with him, graciously give us all things? Romans 8:31–32

MOMENTS FOR RENEWAL

Loving Father, teach me to trust in your goodness—not just when I'm good, but all the time.

44

Family Trademarks

Read 1 John 4:7-16

The Aran Islands, off the west coast of Ireland, are known for their beautiful sweaters. Patterns are woven into the fabric using sheep's wool to craft the garments. Many of them relate to the culture and folklore of these small islands, but some are more personal. Each family on the islands has its own trademark pattern, which is so distinctive that if a fisherman were to drown it is said that he could be identified simply by examining his sweater for the family trademark.

In John's first letter, the apostle describes things that are to be trademarks of those who are members of God's family. In 1 John 3:1, John affirms that we are indeed part of God's family by saying, "See what great love the Father has lavished on us, that we should be called children of God!" He then describes the trademarks of those who are the children of God, including, "Dear friends, let us love one another, for love comes from God. Everyone who loves has been born of God and knows God" (4:7).

Because "love comes from God," the chief way to reflect the heart of the Father is by displaying the love that characterizes Him. May we allow His love to reach out to others through us—for love is one of our family trademarks.

MOMENTS FOR REFLECTION

We love because he first loved us. 1 John 4:19

A new command I give you: Love one another. As I have loved you, so you must love one another. By this everyone will know that you are my disciples, if you love one another. John 13:34–35

Let no debt remain outstanding, except the continuing debt to love one another. Romans 13:8

MOMENTS FOR RENEWAL

Father, help me rest in your love so that your love for me will naturally overflow to those around me.

45

He Found Me

Read Luke 19:1-10

The film *Amazing Grace* was set in the late 1700s. It tells the story of William Wilberforce, a politician who was driven by his faith in Christ to commit his money and energy to abolishing the slave trade in England. In one scene, Wilberforce's butler finds him praying. The butler asks, "You found God, sir?" Wilberforce responds, "I think He found me."

The Bible pictures humanity as wayward and wandering sheep. It says, "We all, like sheep, have gone astray, each of us has turned to our own way" (Isaiah 53:6). In fact, this wayward condition is so deeply rooted in us that the apostle Paul said: "There is no one righteous, not even one; there is no one who understands; there is no one who seeks God. All have turned away" (Romans 3:10–12). That is why Jesus came. We would never seek Him, so He came seeking us. Jesus declared His mission with the words, "For the Son of Man came to seek and to save the lost" (Luke 19:10).

Wilberforce was exactly right. Jesus came to find us, for we could never have found Him if left to ourselves. It is a clear expression of the Creator's love for His lost creation that He pursues us and desires to make us His own.

MOMENTS FOR REFLECTION

The Son of Man came to seek and to save the lost.
Luke 19:10

If a man has a hundred sheep and one of them gets
lost, what will he do? Won't he leave the ninety-nine
others in the wilderness and go to search for the one
that is lost until he finds it? . . . He will call together
his friends and neighbors, saying, "Rejoice with me
because I have found my lost sheep." Luke 15:4, 6 NLT

There is joy in the presence of God's angels when
even one sinner repents. Luke 15:10 NLT

MOMENTS FOR RENEWAL

*Father, I'm thankful you came to seek and to save the lost. As I go about
my day today, help me to remember your generous mercy and your unchanging love for me.*

46

Here for You

Read Deuteronomy 15:7–11

On the outskirts of Paris, as in other cities around the globe, people are coming to the aid of the homeless in their communities. Clothing, covered in waterproof bags, is hung on designated fences for those living on the streets to take according to their needs. The bags are labeled, "I'm not lost; I'm for you if you're cold." The effort not only warms those without shelter, but also teaches those in the community the importance of assisting the needy among them.

The Bible highlights the importance of caring for those who are poor, instructing us to be "openhanded" toward them (Deuteronomy 15:11). We might be tempted to avert our eyes to the plight of the poor, holding tightly to our resources instead of sharing them. Yet God challenges us to recognize that we will always be surrounded by those who have needs and therefore to respond to them with generosity, not a "grudging heart" (v. 10). Jesus says that in giving to the poor we receive an enduring treasure in heaven (Luke 12:33).

Our generosity may not be recognized by anyone other than God. Yet when we give freely, we not only meet the needs of those around us but we also experience the joy God intends for us in providing for others. Help us, Lord, to have open eyes and open hands to supply the needs of those You place in our paths!

> I command you to be openhanded toward your fellow Israelites who are poor and needy in your land.
>
> Deuteronomy 15:11

> Whoever oppresses the poor shows contempt for their Maker, but whoever is kind to the needy honors God. Proverbs 14:31

> Owe no one anything except to love one another, for he who loves another has fulfilled the law.
>
> Romans 13:8 NKJV

MOMENTS FOR RENEWAL

With Jesus, reflect on your financial giving this year. Ask your Savior if there is a particular person (or ministry or cause) to whom you should consider giving.

47

To Be Continued

Read Acts 1:1–11

The fifth book of the New Testament, the Acts of the Apostles—abbreviated to Acts—records the beginnings of the Christian church under the leadership of the people Jesus had appointed. Some suggest this book could also be called the *Acts of the Holy Spirit*, because the Spirit's power supplied courage for the apostles in the face of every struggle.

Just before Jesus was taken up into heaven, He told the ones He had chosen: "You will receive power when the Holy Spirit comes on you; and you will be my witnesses in Jerusalem, and in all Judea and Samaria, and to the ends of the earth" (Acts 1:8). With those words, one chapter in the story of God's work on Earth ended, and a new one began. We are a part of that ongoing story.

The book of Acts describes the faithful witness of Peter, John, Barnabas, Paul, Tabitha, Lydia, and many others during the early days of the church. These ordinary people depended on God to give them strength as they spread His Word and demonstrated His love.

That story continues through us. As we trust God and obey His direction to make Jesus known, He writes through us new pages in His story of redemption.

But you will receive power when the Holy Spirit comes on you; and you will be my witnesses in Jerusalem, and in all Judea and Samaria, and to the ends of the earth. Acts 1:8

By faith these people overthrew kingdoms, ruled with justice, and received what God had promised them. They shut the mouths of lions, quenched the flames of fire, and escaped death by the edge of the sword. Their weakness was turned to strength. Hebrews 11:33–34 NLT

I am the vine, you are the branches. He who abides in Me, and I in him, bears much fruit. John 15:5 NKJV

MOMENTS FOR RENEWAL

Gracious Spirit, without you, I would be powerless to please God. Open my eyes to your work and life in me. Help me be sensitive to your promptings and direction.

48

God at Work

Read Matthew 27:50-54

*G*od is crying." Those were the words whispered by Bill Haley's ten-year-old daughter as she stood in the rain with a group of multiethnic believers in Jesus. They had come to Virginia's Shenandoah Valley to seek God and make sense of the legacy of racial discord in America. As they stood on the grounds where former slaves were buried, they joined hands in prayer. Then suddenly the wind began to blow, and it started to rain. As the leader called out for racial healing, the rain began to fall even harder. Those gathered believed that God was at work to bring reconciliation and forgiveness.

And so was it at Calvary—God was at work. After the crucified Jesus breathed His last, "The earth shook, the rocks split and the tombs broke open" (Matthew 27:51–52). Though some had denied who Jesus was, a centurion assigned to guard Him had come to a different conclusion: "When the centurion and those with him . . . saw the earthquake and all that had happened, they were terrified, and exclaimed, 'Surely he was the Son of God!'" (v. 54).

In the death of Jesus, God was at work providing forgiveness of sin for all who believe in Him. "God was reconciling the world to himself in Christ, not counting people's sins against them" (2 Corinthians 5:19). And what better way to demonstrate that we've been forgiven by God than to extend forgiveness to each other.

> At that moment the curtain in the sanctuary of the Temple was torn in two, from top to bottom. The earth shook, rocks split apart, and tombs opened.
>
> Matthew 27:51–52 NLT

> He has committed to [you] the message of reconciliation. 2 Corinthians 5:19

> Beloved, let us love one another, for love is of God; and everyone who loves is born of God and knows God. 1 John 4:7 NKJV

MOMENTS FOR RENEWAL

Father, thank you for loving the world so much that you sent Jesus so that I can be forgiven. Help me follow your example by extending forgiveness to others.

49

Plodding for God

Read Hebrews 6:9-12

Those raised in the English village with William Carey (1761–1834) probably thought he wouldn't accomplish much, but today he's known as the father of modern missions. Born to parents who were weavers, he became a not-too successful teacher and cobbler while teaching himself Greek, Hebrew, and Latin. After many years, he realized his dream of becoming a missionary to India. But he faced hardship, including his child's death, his wife's mental-health problems, and for many years the lack of response from those he served.

What kept him serving amid difficulties as he translated the entire Bible into six languages and parts of it into twenty-nine others? "I can plod," he said. "I can persevere in any definite pursuit." He committed to serving God no matter what trials he encountered.

This continued devotion to Christ is what the writer to the Hebrews counseled. He called for those reading his letter to not "become lazy" (Hebrews 6:12), but to "show this same diligence to the very end" (v. 11) as they sought to honor God. He reassured them that God "will not forget your work and the love you have shown" (v. 10).

During William Carey's later years, he reflected on how God consistently supplied his needs. "He has never failed in His promise, so I cannot fail in my service to Him." May God also empower us to serve Him day by day.

MOMENTS FOR REFLECTION

We want each of you to show this same diligence to the very end. Hebrews 6:11

Therefore we do not lose heart. Though outwardly we are wasting away, yet inwardly we are being renewed day by day. 2 Corinthians 4:16

That you may love the LORD your God, listen to his voice, and hold fast to him. For the LORD is your life. Deuteronomy 30:20

MOMENTS FOR RENEWAL

Ask your Savior for the gift of perseverance in an area in which you struggle. Listen for His loving response to you.

50

Living Bridges

Read Jeremiah 17:5-10

People who live in Cherrapunji, India, have developed a unique way to get across the many rivers and streams in their land. They grow bridges from the roots of rubber trees. These "living bridges" take between ten and fifteen years to mature, but once they are established, they are extremely stable and last for hundreds of years.

The Bible compares a person who trusts in God to "a tree planted by the water that sends out its roots by the stream" (Jeremiah 17:8). Because its roots are well-nourished, this tree survives soaring temperatures. And during drought it continues to yield fruit.

Like a firmly rooted tree, people who rely on God have a sense of stability and vitality despite the worst circumstances. In contrast, people who place their trust in other humans often live with a sense of instability. The Bible compares them to desert shrubs that are frequently malnourished and stand alone (v. 6). So it is with the spiritual lives of people who forsake God.

Where are our roots? Are we rooted in Jesus? (Colossians 2:7). Are we a bridge that leads others to Him? If we know Christ, we can testify to this truth: Blessed are those who trust in the Lord (Jeremiah 17:7).

But blessed is the one who trusts in the LORD, whose confidence is in him. They will be like a tree planted by the water that sends out its roots by the stream. It does not fear when heat comes; its leaves are always green. It has no worries in a year of drought and never fails to bear fruit. Jeremiah 17:7–8

Remain in me, as I also remain in you. No branch can bear fruit by itself; it must remain in the vine. Neither can you bear fruit unless you remain in me. John 15:4

MOMENTS FOR RENEWAL

Father, help me abide in you, rest in your strength, and call out to you in any and every situation. Thank you for the promise of a fruitful life when living in dependence on you.

51

Listening Matters

Read Psalm 85

ome at once. We have struck a berg." Those were the first words
Harold Cottam, the wireless operator on the RMS *Carpathia*,
received from the sinking RMS *Titanic* at 12:25 a.m. on April
15, 1912. The *Carpathia* would be the first ship to the disaster scene,
saving 706 lives.

In the US Senate hearings days later, the *Carpathia's* captain Arthur
Rostron testified, "The whole thing was absolutely providential. . . .
The wireless operator was in his cabin at the time, not on official business at all, but just simply listening as he was undressing. . . . In ten
minutes maybe he would have been in bed, and we would not have
heard the message."

Listening matters—especially listening to God. The writers of
Psalm 85, the sons of Korah, urged attentive obedience when they
wrote, "I will listen to what God the LORD says; he promises peace to
his people, his faithful servants—but let them not turn to folly. Surely
his salvation is near those who fear him" (vv. 8–9). Their admoni-
tion is especially poignant because their ancestor Korah had rebelled
against God and had perished in the wilderness (Numbers 16:1–35).

The night the *Titanic* sank, another ship was much closer, but its
wireless operator had gone to bed. Had he heard the distress signal,
perhaps more lives would have been saved. When we listen to God by

obeying His teaching, He'll help us navigate even life's most troubled waters.

MOMENTS FOR REFLECTION

My sheep listen to my voice; I know them, and they follow me. John 10:27

If my people, who are called by my name, will humble themselves and pray and seek my face and turn from their wicked ways, then I will hear from heaven, and I will forgive their sin and will heal their land.
2 Chronicles 7:14

Do not merely listen to the word, and so deceive yourselves. Do what it says. James 1:22

MOMENTS FOR RENEWAL

Father, help me to stay close to you in my thoughts, words, and actions. Please use me as your servant to bring your hope to others.

52

Gray Power

Read Joshua 14:6-12

Dutch artist Yoni Lefevre created a project called "Gray Power" to show the vitality of the aging generation in the Netherlands. She asked local schoolchildren to sketch their grandparents. Lefevre wanted to show an "honest and pure view" of older people, and she believed children could help supply this. The youngsters' drawings reflected a fresh and lively perspective of their elders—grandmas and grandpas were shown playing tennis, gardening, painting, and more!

Caleb, of ancient Israel, was vital into his senior years. As a young man, he infiltrated the promised land before the Israelites conquered it. Caleb believed God would help his nation defeat the Canaanites, but the other spies disagreed (Joshua 14:8). Because of Caleb's faith, God miraculously sustained his life for forty-five years so he might survive the wilderness wanderings and enter the promised land. When it was finally time to enter Canaan, eighty-five-year-old Caleb said, "I am still as strong today as the day Moses sent me out" (v. 11). With God's help, Caleb successfully claimed his share of the land (Numbers 14:24).

God does not forget about us as we grow older. Although our bodies age and our health may fail, God's Holy Spirit renews us inwardly each day (2 Corinthians 4:16). He makes it possible for our lives to have significance at every stage and every age.

MOMENTS FOR REFLECTION

Today I am eighty-five years old. I am as strong now as I was when Moses sent me on that journey, and I can still travel and fight as well as I could then. So give me the hill country that the LORD promised me.

Joshua 14:10–12 NLT

Because my servant Caleb has a different spirit and follows me wholeheartedly, I will bring him into the land he went to, and his descendants will inherit it.

Numbers 14:24

That is why we never give up. Though our bodies are dying, our spirits are being renewed every day.

2 Corinthians 4:16 NLT

MOMENTS FOR RENEWAL

Father, I know that my physical strength and health can fail. But I pray that you will continually renew me spiritually so I can serve you faithfully as long as I live.

53

Spending Time with God

Read Luke 5:12-16

A River Runs through It is Norman Maclean's masterful story of two boys growing up in western Montana with their father, a Presbyterian minister. On Sunday mornings, Norman and his brother, Paul, went to church where they heard their father preach. Once Sunday evening rolled around, there was another service and their father would preach again. But between those two services, they were free to walk the hills and streams with him "while he unwound between services." It was an intentional withdrawing on their father's part to "restore his soul and be filled again to overflowing for the evening sermon."

Throughout the Gospels, Jesus is seen teaching multitudes on hillsides and cities, and healing the sick and diseased who were brought to Him. All this interaction was in line with the Son of Man's mission "to seek and to save the lost" (Luke 19:10). But it's also noted that He "often withdrew to lonely places" (5:16). His time there was spent communing with the Father, being renewed and restored to step back once more into His mission.

In our faithful efforts to serve, it's good for us to remember that Jesus "often" withdrew. If this practice was important for Jesus, how much more so for us? May we regularly spend time with our Father, who can fill us again to overflowing.

MOMENTS FOR REFLECTION

Jesus often withdrew to lonely places and prayed.

Luke 5:16

Keep me as the apple of your eye; hide me in the shadow of your wings. Psalm 17:8

I have seen you in your sanctuary and gazed upon your power and glory. Your unfailing love is better than life itself; how I praise you! Psalm 63:2–3 NLT

MOMENTS FOR RENEWAL

Father, thank you for the reminder of my need for time spent with you. I need your grace and strength to renew my often-weary soul.

54

Walking with the Spirit

Read Galatians 5:13–18

Ten thousand hours. That's how long author Malcolm Gladwell suggests it takes to become skillful at any craft. Even for the greatest artists and musicians of all time, their tremendous inborn talent wasn't enough to achieve the level of expertise that they would eventually attain. They needed to immerse themselves in their craft every single day.

As strange as it might seem, we need a similar mentality when it comes to learning to live in the power of the Holy Spirit. In Galatians, Paul encourages the church to be set apart for God. But Paul explained that this couldn't be achieved through merely obeying a set of rules. Instead we're called to walk with the Holy Spirit. The Greek word that Paul uses for "walk" in Galatians 5:16 literally means to "walk around and around something," or "to journey" (*peripateo*). So for Paul, walking with the Spirit meant journeying with the Spirit each day—it's not just a one-time experience of His power.

May we pray to be filled with the Spirit daily—to yield to the Spirit's work as He counsels, guides, comforts, and is simply there with us. And as we're "led by the Spirit" in this way (v. 18), we become better and better at hearing His voice and following His leading. *Holy Spirit, may we walk with you today, and every day!*

Walk by the Spirit, and you will not gratify the desires of the flesh. For the flesh desires what is contrary to the Spirit, and the Spirit what is contrary to the flesh. They are in conflict with each other, so that you are not to do whatever you want. But if you are led by the Spirit, you are not under the law. Galatians 5:16–18

Now the Lord is the Spirit, and where the Spirit of the Lord is, there is freedom. 2 Corinthians 3:17

The fruit of the Spirit is love, joy, peace, forbearance, kindness, goodness, faithfulness, gentleness and self-control. Against such things there is no law.

Galatians 5:22–23

MOMENTS FOR RENEWAL

Ask God what spiritual fruit the Spirit is instilling in you during this season, and listen for His loving response.

55

Peace in the Chaos

Read Psalm 121

omething that sounded like firecrackers roused Joanne from sleep. Glass shattered. Wishing she didn't live alone, she got up to see what was going on. The dark streets were empty and the house seemed to be OK—then she saw the broken mirror.

Investigators found a bullet only a half-inch from the gas line. If it had struck the line, she probably wouldn't have made it out alive. Later they discovered it was a stray bullet from nearby apartments, but now Joanne was afraid to be at home. She prayed for peace, and once the glass was cleaned up, her heart calmed.

Psalm 121 is a reminder for us to look to God in times of trouble. Here, we see that we can have peace and calm because our "help comes from the LORD, the Maker of heaven and earth" (v. 2). The God who created the universe helps and watches over us (v. 3)—even while we sleep—but He himself never sleeps (v. 4). He watches over us day and night (v. 6), "both now and forevermore" (v. 8).

No matter what kind of situations we find ourselves in, God sees. And He's waiting for us to turn to Him. When we do, our circumstances may not always change, but He's promised His peace in the midst of it all.

The LORD will keep you from all harm—he will watch over your life; the LORD will watch over your coming and going both now and forevermore. Psalm 121:7–8

Have I not commanded you? Be strong and courageous. Do not be afraid; do not be discouraged, for the LORD your God will be with you wherever you go. Joshua 1:9

May your unfailing love be my comfort, according to your promise to [me]. Psalm 119:76

MOMENTS FOR RENEWAL

Father, thank you for your peace. Please continue to calm my heart in the areas of my life that feel chaotic.

56

A Worthwhile Wait

Read Isaiah 30:15-19

Stuck in a stressful job with long hours and an unreasonable boss, James wished he could quit. But he had a mortgage, a wife, and a young child to take care of. He was tempted to resign anyway, but his wife reminded him: "Let's hang on and see what God will give us."

Many months later, their prayers were answered. James found a new job that he enjoyed and gave him more time with the family. "Those months were long," he told me, "but I'm glad I waited for God's plan to unfold in His time."

Waiting for God's help in the midst of trouble is hard; it can be tempting to try to find our own solution first. The Israelites did just that: under threat from their enemies, they sought help from Egypt instead of turning to God (Isaiah 30:2). But God told them: if only they would repent and put their trust in Him, they would find strength and salvation (v. 15). In fact, He added, "the LORD longs to be gracious to you" (v. 18).

Waiting for God takes faith and patience. But when we see His answer at the end of it all, we'll realize it was worth it: "Blessed are all who wait for him!" (v. 18). And what's even more amazing, God is waiting for us to come to Him!

MOMENTS FOR REFLECTION

Therefore the LORD longs to be gracious to you, and therefore He waits on high to have compassion on you. For the LORD is a God of justice; how blessed are all those who long for Him. Isaiah 30:18 NASB

Wait on the LORD; be of good courage, and He shall strengthen your heart; wait, I say, on the LORD! Psalm 27:14 NKJV

Trust in the LORD with all your heart and lean not on your own understanding; in all your ways submit to him, and he will make your paths straight. Proverbs 3:5–6

MOMENTS FOR RENEWAL

Father, give me the patience to wait for your answer. I know you're a good and loving God whose timing and will are always perfect.

57

The New Normal

Read Hebrews 4:9-16

pastor, who was trained in trauma and grief counseling, com-
mented that the greatest challenge for people who are hurting
is often not the immediate heartache of the loss. Instead, the
biggest problem is adjusting to the different kind of life that follows.
What once was normal may never be normal again. So the challenge
for those offering help is to assist the sufferers as they establish the
"new normal." It may be a new normal that no longer includes robust
health, a treasured relationship, or a satisfying job. Or it may be living without a loved one who has been taken in death. The gravity of
such losses forces us to live a different kind of life—no matter how
unwelcome it may be.

When our "new normal" comes, it's easy to think no one understands how we feel. But that isn't true. Part of the reason Jesus came
was to experience life among us, resulting in His present ministry:
"For we do not have a high priest who is unable to empathize with
our weaknesses, but we have one who has been tempted in every way,
just as we are—yet he did not sin" (Hebrews 4:15).

Our Savior lived a perfect life, yet He also knew the pains of a
broken world. He endured sorrow; He suffered agony. And He stands
ready to encourage us when the dark moments of life force us to embrace a new normal.

MOMENTS FOR REFLECTION

Jesus wept. John 11:35

He was oppressed and treated harshly, yet he never said a word. Isaiah 53:7 NLT

We do not have a high priest who is unable to empathize with our weaknesses, but we have one who has been tempted in every way, just as we are—yet he did not sin. Hebrews 4:15

MOMENTS FOR RENEWAL

Ponder the mystery and miracle of having a God who enters into your pain and suffering, and tell Jesus what that means to you. Listen for His loving response.

58

Practicing What We Preach

Read 1 John 2:7-11

Pastor and writer Eugene Peterson had the opportunity to hear a lecture by Swiss physician and highly respected pastoral counselor Paul Tournier. Peterson had read the doctor's works, and admired his approach to healing. The lecture left a deep impression on Peterson. As he listened, he had the feeling that Tournier lived what he spoke and spoke what he lived. Peterson chose this word to describe his experience: "Congruence. It is the best word I can come up with."

Congruence—it's what some refer to as "practicing what you preach" or "walking your talk." The apostle John stresses that if any of us "claims to be in the light but hates a brother or sister," then we're "still in the darkness" (1 John 2:9). In essence, our lives and our words simply don't match up. John goes further to say such people "do not know where they are going" (v. 11). The word he chose to describe how incongruence leaves us? Blind.

Living closely aligned to God by allowing the light of His Word to illuminate our paths keeps us from living blind. The result is a godly vision that gives clarity and focus to our days—our words and actions match up. When others observe this, the impression is not necessarily that of someone who knows everywhere they're going, but of someone who clearly knows who they're following.

> Anyone who claims to be in the light but hates a brother or sister is still in the darkness. 1 John 2:9

> Search me, O God, and know my heart; test me and know my anxious thoughts. Point out anything in me that offends you, and lead me along the path of everlasting life. Psalm 139:23–24 NLT

> The purposes of a person's heart are deep waters, but one who has insight draws them out. Proverbs 20:5

Jesus, I want to live a life where my words and actions match up. There are times I fall short, but my desire is to grow more consistent with each passing day. Help me, please, so that everyone listening and watching my life will be drawn to you.

59

Eureka Stone

Read Matthew 13:44–50

I n 1867 on a farm in South Africa, fifteen-year-old Erasmus Jacobs saw a stone glistening in the sun. The shining rock was eventually reported to a neighbor, who wanted to buy it from the family. Not knowing its value, Erasmus's mother told the neighbor, "You can keep the stone, if you want it."

Eventually, a mineralogist determined the stone to be a 21.25 carat diamond and worth a great sum. It became known as the *Eureka Diamond*. (The Greek word *eureka* means "I found it!") Soon the fields near the Jacobs' farm soared in value. Underneath the land was one of the richest diamond deposits ever discovered.

Jesus said that the value of being part of God's kingdom is like treasure: "The kingdom of heaven is like treasure hidden in a field. When a man found it, he hid it again, and then in his joy went and sold all he had and bought that field" (Matthew 13:44).

When we put our faith in Christ, a spiritual "eureka moment" arrives. God gives us forgiveness in His Son. It is the greatest treasure that could ever be found. Now all of life can begin to center on the value of becoming a joyous member of His eternal kingdom. It's our joy to share that valuable discovery with others.

The kingdom of heaven is like treasure hidden in a field. When a man found it, he hid it again, and then in his joy went and sold all he had and bought that field. Matthew 13:44

Having chosen them, he called them to come to him. And having called them, he gave them right standing with himself. And having given them right standing, he gave them his glory. Romans 8:30 NLT

The Kingdom of God is within you. Luke 17:21 GNT

MOMENTS FOR RENEWAL

Jesus, thank you for inviting me into your eternal kingdom. Help me live in the light of that beautiful reality today.

60

Just a Touch

Read Revelation 1:9–18

I t was just a touch, but it made all the difference to Colin. As his small team was preparing to do charitable work in a region known for hostility to believers in Jesus, his stress level began to rise. When he shared his worries with a teammate, his friend stopped, placed his hand on his shoulder, and shared a few encouraging words with him. Colin now looks back on that brief touch as a turning point, a powerful reminder of the simple truth that God was with him.

John, the close friend and disciple of Jesus, had been banished to the desolate island of Patmos for preaching the gospel, when he heard "a loud voice like a trumpet" (Revelation 1:10). That startling event was followed by a vision of the Lord Himself, and John "fell at his feet as though dead." But in that frightening moment, he received comfort and courage. John wrote, "He placed his right hand on me and said, 'Do not be afraid. I am the First and the Last'" (v. 17).

God takes us out of our comfort zone to show us new things, to stretch us, to help us grow. But He also brings the courage and comfort to go through every situation. He won't leave us alone in our trials. He has everything under control. He has us in His hands.

Then he placed his right hand on me and said: "Do not be afraid. I am the First and the Last." Revelation 1:17

The LORD replied, "My Presence will go with you, and I will give you rest." Exodus 33:14

And Jesus came and spoke to them, saying, "All authority has been given to Me in heaven and on earth. . . . and lo, I am with you always, even to the end of the age." Matthew 28:18, 20 NKJV

MOMENTS FOR RENEWAL

Father, help me recognize your presence even when I'm anxious or afraid.

61

Bring What You Have

Read John 6:4–14

S tone Soup," an old tale with many versions, tells of a starving man who comes to a village, but no one there can spare a crumb of food for him. He puts a stone and water in a pot over a fire. Intrigued, the villagers watch him as he begins to stir his "soup." Eventually, one brings a couple of potatoes to add to the mix; another has a few carrots. One person adds an onion, another a handful of barley. A farmer donates some milk. Eventually, the "stone soup" becomes a tasty chowder.

That tale illustrates the value of sharing, but it also reminds us to bring what we have, even when it seems to be insignificant. In John 6:1–14 we read of a boy who appears to be the only person in a huge crowd who thought about bringing some food. Jesus's disciples had little use for the boy's sparse lunch of five loaves and two fishes. But when it was surrendered, Jesus increased it and fed thousands of hungry people!

Just as Jesus took one person's meal and multiplied it far beyond anyone's expectations or imagination (v. 11), He'll accept our surrendered efforts, talents, and service. He just wants us to be willing to bring what we have to Him.

"Bring them here to me," [Jesus] said. Matthew 14:18

But he said to me, "My grace is sufficient for you, for my power is made perfect in weakness." 2 Corinthians 12:9

Consecrate yourselves, for tomorrow the LORD will do amazing things among you. Joshua 3:5

MOMENTS FOR RENEWAL

With Jesus, take inventory of the talents, resources, and skills that He's entrusted to you. Ask Christ what He wants you to know about each one.

62

A Purpose in Pain?

Read 2 Corinthians 1:3-7

When Siu Fen discovered she had kidney failure and would need dialysis for the rest of her life, she wanted to give up. Retired and single, the longtime believer in Jesus saw no point in prolonging her life. But friends convinced her to persevere and go for dialysis and trust in God to help her.

Two years later, she found her experience coming into play when she visited a friend from church with a debilitating disease. The woman felt alone, as few could truly understand what she was going through. But Siu Fen was able to identify with her physical and emotional pain and could connect with her in a personal way. Her own journey enabled her to walk alongside the woman, giving her a special measure of comfort others couldn't. "Now I see how God can still use me," she said.

It can be hard to understand why we suffer. Yet God can use our affliction in unexpected ways. As we turn to Him for comfort and love in the midst of trials, it also empowers us to help others. No wonder Paul learned to see purpose in his own suffering: It gave him the opportunity to receive God's comfort, which he could then use to bless others (2 Corinthians 1:3–5). We're not asked to deny our pain and suffering, but we can take heart in God's ability to use it for good.

[God] comforts us in all our troubles, so that we can comfort those in any trouble with the comfort we ourselves receive from God. 2 Corinthians 1:4

Surely He has borne our griefs and carried our sorrows. Isaiah 53:4 NKJV

The LORD is close to the brokenhearted and saves those who are crushed in spirit. Psalm 34:18

MOMENTS FOR RENEWAL

Father, help me to keep trusting in you in the midst of trouble, knowing that I can tap your unlimited comfort and share it with others.

63

A Great Light

Read Isaiah 9:1–3

In 2018, twelve Thai boys and their soccer coach descended into a mazelike cave, intending to enjoy an afternoon adventure. Due to unexpected rising water that forced them deeper and deeper into the cavern, it was two-and-a-half weeks before rescuers led them out. Dive teams, thwarted by rising water, attempted the rescue as the boys sat on a small rock shelf with only six flickering flashlights. They spent hours in darkness, hoping that somehow light—and help— would break through.

The prophet Isaiah described a world of brooding darkness, one overrun by violence and greed, shattered by rebellion and anguish (Isaiah 8:22). Nothing but ruin; hope's candle flickering and fading, sputtering before succumbing to dark nothingness. And yet, Isaiah insisted, this dim despair was not the end. Because of God's mercy, soon "there will be no more gloom for those who were in distress" (9:1). God would never abandon His people in shadowy ruin. The prophet announced hope for his people then and pointed to the time when Jesus would come to dispel the darkness sin has caused.

Jesus has come. And now we hear Isaiah's words with renewed meaning: "The people walking in darkness have seen a great light," Isaiah says. "On those living in the land of deep darkness a light has dawned" (v. 2).

No matter how dark the night, no matter how despairing our circumstances, we're never forsaken in the dark. Jesus is here. A great Light shines.

MOMENTS FOR REFLECTION

A light has dawned. Isaiah 9:2

In [Jesus] was life, and that life was the light of all mankind. John 1:4

I am the light of the world. If you follow me, you won't have to walk in darkness, because you will have the light that leads to life. John 8:12 NLT

MOMENTS FOR RENEWAL

Father, there's so much darkness. I fear sometimes that the darkness will overwhelm me. Be my great light. Shine on me with radiant love.

64

Waiting for a Blessing

Read Habakkuk 1:12–2:4

A popular restaurant in Bangkok serves soup from a broth that has been cooking for forty-five years and is replenished a bit each day. The practice, called "perpetual stew," dates back to medieval times. Just as some "leftovers" taste better a few days later, the extended cooking time blends and creates unique flavors. The restaurant has won multiple awards for the most delicious broth in Thailand.

Good things often take time, but our human nature struggles with patience. The question "How long?" occurs throughout the Bible. One poignant example is from the prophet Habakkuk, who begins his book by asking, "How long, LORD, must I call for help, but you do not listen?" (Habakkuk 1:2). Habakkuk (whose name means "grappler") prophesied God's judgment on his country (Judah) through the invasion of the ruthless Babylonian Empire, and he wrestled with how God could allow corrupt people to prosper as they exploited others. But God promised hope and restoration in His own time: "For the revelation [of God's help] awaits an appointed time. . . . Though it linger, wait for it; it will certainly come and will not delay" (2:3).

The Babylonian captivity lasted seventy years. By human reckoning that's a long time, but God is always faithful and true to His Word.

Some of God's best blessings may be long in coming. Though they linger, keep looking to Him! He prepares every blessing with perfect wisdom and care—and He's always worth waiting for.

MOMENTS FOR REFLECTION

> Though it linger, wait for it. Habakkuk 2:3

> In the morning, Lord, you hear my voice; in the morning I lay my requests before you and wait expectantly. Psalm 5:3

> The Lord is good to those whose hope is in him, to the one who seeks him; it is good to wait quietly for the salvation of the Lord. Lamentations 3:25–26

MOMENTS FOR RENEWAL

How is God inviting you to look to Him with expectation during this time? Ask your heavenly Father for the courage, faith, and strength to wait on Him, no matter what. Listen for His response to your prayer.

65

Live. Pray. Love.

Read Romans 12:9-21

Influenced by parents who were strong believers in Jesus, track star Jesse Owens lived as a courageous man of faith. During the 1936 Olympic Games in Berlin, Owens, one of the few African Americans on the US team, received four gold medals in the presence of hate-filled Nazis and their leader, Hitler. He also befriended fellow athlete Luz Long, a German. Owens's simple act of living out his faith while surrounded by Nazi propaganda impacted Luz's life. Later, Long wrote to Owens: "That hour in Berlin when I first spoke to you, when you had your knee upon the ground, I knew you were in prayer. . . . I think I might believe in God."

Owens demonstrated how believers can answer the apostle Paul's charge to "hate what is evil" and be "devoted to one another in love" (Romans 12:9–10). Though he could have responded to the evil around him with hate, Owens chose to live by faith and show love to a man who would later become his friend and eventually consider belief in God.

As God's people commit to being "faithful in prayer" (v. 12), He empowers us to "live in harmony with one another" (v. 16).

When we depend on prayer, we can commit to living out our faith and loving all who are made in God's image. As we cry out to God, He'll help us break down barriers and build bridges of peace with our neighbors.

Love must be sincere. Hate what is evil; cling to what is good. Be devoted to one another in love. Honor one another above yourselves. Romans 12:9–10

Regard no one from a worldly point of view. . . . If anyone is in Christ, the new creation has come: The old has gone, the new is here! All this is from God, who reconciled us to himself through Christ and gave us the ministry of reconciliation. 2 Corinthians 5:16–18

A new command I give you: Love one another.
John 13:34

MOMENTS FOR RENEWAL

Father, please strengthen us to come together in prayer, fully committed to loving others and living peacefully.

66

When We Praise

Read Acts 16:25–34

When nine-year-old Willie was abducted from his front yard in 2014, he sang his favorite gospel song "Every Praise" over and over again. During the three-hour ordeal, Willie ignored the kidnapper's repeated orders to keep silent as they drove around. Eventually, the kidnapper let Willie out of the car unharmed. Later, Willie described the encounter, saying that while he felt his fear give way to faith, the abductor seemed agitated by the song.

Willie's response to his dire situation is reminiscent of the experience shared by Paul and Silas. After being flogged and thrown into jail, they reacted by "praying and singing hymns to God, and the other prisoners were listening to them. Suddenly there was such a violent earthquake that the foundations of the prison were shaken. At once all the prison doors flew open, and everyone's chains came loose" (Acts 16:25–26).

Upon witnessing this awesome demonstration of power, the jailer believed in the God of Paul and Silas, and his entire household was baptized along with him (vv. 27–34). Through the avenue of praise, both physical and spiritual chains were broken that night.

We may not always experience a visibly dramatic rescue like Paul and Silas, or like Willie. But we know that God responds to the praises of His people! When He moves, chains fall apart.

At once all the prison doors flew open, and every-one's chains came loose. Acts 16:26

They confronted me in the day of my disaster, but the Lord was my support. He brought me out into a spacious place; he rescued me because he delighted in me. Psalm 18:18–19

You are worthy, O Lord our God, to receive glory and honor and power. For you created all things, and they exist because you created what you pleased.

Revelation 4:11 NLT

MOMENTS FOR RENEWAL

If you can, take a couple of moments to praise God in whatever way you most enjoy—whether listening to worship music, journaling your prayers, or walking outside to behold His creation. As you do, listen for His joy in your worship, and in you.

67

Mercy's Lament

Read Lamentations 2:10-13, 18-19

Her father blamed his illness on witchcraft. It was AIDS. When he died, his daughter, ten-year-old Mercy, grew even closer to her mother. But her mother was sick too, and three years later she died. From then on, Mercy's sister raised the five siblings. That's when Mercy began to keep a journal of her deep pain.

The prophet Jeremiah kept a record of his pain too. In the grim book of Lamentations, he wrote of atrocities done to Judah by the Babylonian army. Jeremiah's heart was especially grieved for the youngest victims. "My heart is poured out on the ground," he cried, "because my people are destroyed, because children and infants faint in the streets of the city" (2:11). The people of Judah had a history of ignoring God, but their children were paying the price too. "Their lives ebb away in their mothers' arms," wrote Jeremiah (v. 12).

We might have expected Jeremiah to reject God in the face of such suffering. Instead, he urged the survivors, "Pour out your heart like water in the presence of the Lord. Lift up your hands to him for the lives of your children" (v. 19).

It's good, as Mercy and Jeremiah did, to pour out our hearts to God. Lament is a crucial part of being human. Even when God permits such pain, He grieves with us. Made as we are in His image, He must lament too!

MOMENTS FOR REFLECTION

Arise, cry out in the night, as the watches of the night begin; pour out your heart like water in the presence of the Lord. Lamentations 2:19

Jesus wept. John 11:35

My heart is changed within me; all my compassion is aroused. Hosea 11:8

MOMENTS FOR RENEWAL

If you are in a season of lament, openly present your grief to God. Listen for His loving response to you.

68

Every Breath

Read Ezekiel 37:1–3, 7–10, 14

When Tee Unn came down with a rare autoimmune disease that weakened all his muscles and nearly killed him, he realized that being able to breathe was a gift. For more than a week, a machine had to pump air into his lungs every few seconds, which was a painful part of his treatment.

Tee Unn made a miraculous recovery, and today he reminds himself not to complain about life's challenges. "I'll just take a deep breath," he says, "and thank God I can."

How easy it is to focus on things we need or want, and forget that sometimes the smallest things in life can be the greatest miracles. In Ezekiel's vision (Ezekiel 37:1–14), God showed the prophet that only He could give life to dry bones. Even after tendons, flesh, and skin had appeared, "there was no breath in them" (v. 8). It was only when God gave them breath that they could live again (v. 10).

This vision illustrated God's promise to restore Israel from devastation. It can also be a reminder that anything we have, big or small, is useless unless God gives us breath.

How about thanking God for the simplest blessings in life today? Amid the daily struggle, let's stop occasionally to take a deep breath, and "let everything that has breath praise the Lord" (Psalm 150:6).

MOMENTS FOR REFLECTION

The LORD God formed man of the dust of the ground, and breathed into his nostrils the breath of life; and man became a living being. Genesis 2:7 NKJV

I will make breath enter you, and you will come to life. Ezekiel 37:5

Jesus said, "Peace be with you! As the Father has sent me, I am sending you." And with that he breathed on them and said, "Receive the Holy Spirit." John 20:21–22

MOMENTS FOR RENEWAL

Father, thank you for every breath you've given me. Thank you for the smallest things in life and the greatest miracles of life.

69

Easily Entangled

Read Hebrews 2:17–18; 12:1–2

Soldiers fighting in a sweltering jungle many years ago encountered a frustrating problem. Without warning, a pervasive prickly vine would attach itself to the soldiers' bodies and gear, causing them to be trapped. As they struggled to get free, even more of the plant's tentacles entangled them. The soldiers dubbed the weed the "wait-a-minute" vine because, once entwined and unable to move forward, they were forced to shout out to other members of their team, "Hey, wait a minute, I'm stuck!"

In a similar way, it's hard for followers of Jesus to move forward when we're ensnared by sin. Hebrews 12:1 tells us to "throw off everything that hinders and the sin that so easily entangles" and "run with perseverance." But how do we throw off the sin weighing us down?

Jesus is the only one who can free us from pervasive sin in our lives. May we learn to fix our eyes on Him, our Savior (12:2). Because the Son of God became "fully human in every way," He knows what it's like to be tempted—yet not sin (2:17–18; 4:15). Alone, we may be desperately entwined by our own sin, but God wants us to overcome temptation. It's not through our own strength, but His, that we can "throw off" entangling sin and run after His righteousness (1 Corinthians 10:13).

MOMENTS FOR REFLECTION

And let us run with endurance the race God has set before us. We do this by keeping our eyes on Jesus, the champion who initiates and perfects our faith.

Hebrews 12:1–2 NLT

God is faithful; he will not let you be tempted beyond what you can bear. But when you are tempted, he will also provide a way out so that you can endure it.

1 Corinthians 10:13

[Jesus] is able also to save forever those who come to God through Him, since He always lives to make intercession for them. Hebrews 7:25 NASB

MOMENTS FOR RENEWAL

Jesus, I ask for your help in changing my heart and habits, knowing that it's only by your strength—not mine—that I can overcome the sin that weighs me down. Thank you for your limitless grace and boundless love.

70

Canceled Debts

Read Deuteronomy 15:1-8

In 2009, Los Angeles County stopped charging families for the costs of their children's incarceration. Though no new fees were charged, those with unpaid fees from before the change in policy were still required to settle their debt. Then in 2018 the county canceled all outstanding financial obligations.

For some families, canceling the debt aided greatly in their struggle to survive; no longer having liens on their property or wages being garnished meant they were better able to put food on the table. It was for this kind of hardship that the Lord called for debts to be forgiven every seven years (Deuteronomy 15:2). He didn't want people to be crippled forever by them.

Because the Israelites were forbidden to charge interest on a loan to fellow Israelites (Exodus 22:25), their motives for lending to a neighbor weren't to make a profit, but rather to help those who were enduring hard times, perhaps due to a bad harvest. Debts were to be freely forgiven every seven years. As a result, there would be less poverty among the people (Deuteronomy 15:4).

Today, believers in Jesus aren't bound by these laws. But God might occasionally prompt us to forgive a debt so those who've been struggling can begin afresh as contributing members of society. When we show such mercy and generosity to others, we lift up God's character and give people hope.

The LORD's time for canceling debts has been proclaimed. Deuteronomy 15:2

Peter came to Jesus and asked, "Lord, how many times shall I forgive my brother or sister who sins against me? Up to seven times?"

Jesus answered, "I tell you, not seven times, but seventy-seven times." Matthew 18:21–22

Whoever has this world's goods, and sees his brother in need, and shuts up his heart from him, how does the love of God abide in him? 1 John 3:17 NKJV

MOMENTS FOR RENEWAL

Ask God how He's calling you to be generous with the blessings He's given you. Listen for His loving response.

71

Stay Awake!

Read Matthew 26:36–46

A German bank employee was in the middle of transferring 62.40 euros from a customer's bank account when he accidentally took a power nap at his desk. He dozed off while his finger was on the "2" key, resulting in a 222 million euros (300 million dollars) transfer into the customer's account. The fallout from the mistake included the firing of the employee's colleague who verified the transfer. Although the mistake was caught and corrected, because he wasn't watchful, the sleepy employee's lapse almost became a nightmare for the bank.

Jesus warned His disciples that if they didn't remain alert, they, too, would make a costly mistake. He took them to a place called Gethsemane to spend some time in prayer. As He prayed, Jesus experienced a grief and sadness such as He'd never known in His earthly life. He asked Peter, James, and John to stay awake to pray and "keep watch" with Him (Matthew 26:38), but they fell asleep (vv. 40–41). Their failure to watch and pray would leave them defenseless when the real temptation of denying Him came calling. In the hour of Christ's greatest need, the disciples lacked spiritual vigilance.

May we heed Jesus's words to remain spiritually awake by being more devoted to spending time with Him in prayer. As we do, He'll strengthen us to resist all kinds of temptations and avoid the costly mistake of denying Jesus.

MOMENTS FOR REFLECTION

Watch and pray so that you will not fall into temptation. The spirit is willing, but the flesh is weak.

Matthew 26:41

Stay alert! Watch out for your great enemy, the devil. He prowls around like a roaring lion, looking for someone to devour. 1 Peter 5:8 NLT

Put on the full armor of God, so that when the day of evil comes, you may be able to stand your ground, and after you have done everything, to stand.

Ephesians 6:13

MOMENTS FOR RENEWAL

Ask God if there's an area of your life in which you're spiritually asleep.

72

No Longer Afraid

Read Zephaniah 3:9-17

When the Ethiopian police found her a week after her abduction, three black-maned lions surrounded her, guarding her as though she were their own. Seven men had kidnapped the twelve-year-old girl, carried her into the woods, and beaten her. Miraculously, however, a small pride of lions heard the girl's cries, came running, and chased off the attackers. "[The lions] stood guard until we found her and then they just left her like a gift and went back into the forest," police Sergeant Wondimu told one reporter.

There are days when violence and evil, like that inflicted on this young girl, overpower us, leaving us without hope and terrified. In ancient times, the people of Judah experienced this. They were overrun by ferocious armies and unable to imagine any possibility of escape. Fear consumed them. However, God always renewed His unrelenting presence with His people: "The LORD, the King of Israel, is with you; never again will you fear any harm" (Zephaniah 3:15). Even when our catastrophes result from our own rebellion, God still comes to our rescue: "The LORD your God is with you, the Mighty Warrior who saves" (v. 17).

Whatever troubles overtake us, whatever evils, Jesus—the Lion of Judah—is with us (Revelation 5:5). No matter how alone we feel, our strong Savior is with us. No matter what fears ravage us, our God assures us that He is by our side.

They will eat and lie down and no one will make them afraid. Zephaniah 3:13

You are a lion's cub, Judah; you return from the prey, my son. Like a lion he crouches and lies down, like a lioness—who dares to rouse him? The scepter will not depart from Judah, nor the ruler's staff from between his feet, until he to whom it belongs shall come and the obedience of the nations shall be his. Genesis 49:9–10

They cried out to the LORD in their trouble, and he delivered them from their distress. Psalm 107:6

MOMENTS FOR RENEWAL

Mighty Warrior God, I need you. I need a Mighty Warrior to stand with me and overwhelm my fears. I'm choosing to trust you.

73

Water Where We Need It

Read John 4:7-14

ake Baikal, the world's deepest lake, is vast and magnificent. Measuring one mile deep and nearly 400 miles (636 km) by 49 miles (79 km) across, it contains one-fifth of all the surface fresh water in the world. But this water is largely inaccessible. Lake Baikal is located in Siberia—one of the most remote areas of Russia. With water so desperately needed for much of our planet, it's ironic that such a vast supply of water is tucked away in a place where not many people can access it.

Although Lake Baikal may be remote, there is an endless source of life-giving water that is available and accessible to those who need it most. When at a well in Samaria, Jesus engaged a woman in conversation, probing at the edges of her deep spiritual thirst. The solution to her heart-need? Jesus Himself.

In contrast to the water she had come to draw from the well, Jesus offered something better: "Everyone who drinks this water will be thirsty again, but whoever drinks the water I give them will never thirst. Indeed, the water I give them will become in them a spring of water welling up to eternal life" (John 4:13–14).

Many things promise satisfaction but never fully quench our thirsty hearts. Jesus alone can truly satisfy our spiritual thirst, and His provision is available to everyone, everywhere.

MOMENTS FOR REFLECTION

> Everyone who drinks this water will be thirsty again, but whoever drinks the water I give them will never thirst. Indeed, the water I give them will become in them a spring of water welling up to eternal life. John 4:13–14

> Come, all you who are thirsty, come to the waters.
> Isaiah 55:1

> With joy you will draw water from the wells of salvation. Isaiah 12:3

MOMENTS FOR RENEWAL

Father, thank you for the life you provide and the purpose and meaning you give to me. Teach me to find my truest satisfaction in you and your love.

74

The Joy God Provides

Read Proverbs 15:13–15, 30

When Marcia's out in public, she always tries to smile at others. It's her way of reaching out to people who might need to see a friendly face. Most of the time, she gets a genuine smile in return. But during a time when Marcia was mandated to wear a face mask, she realized that people could no longer see her mouth, thus no one could see her smile. It's sad, she thought, but I'm not going to stop. Maybe they'll see in my eyes that I'm smiling.

There's actually a bit of science behind that idea. The muscles for the corners of the mouth and the ones that make the eyes crinkle can work in tandem. It's called a Duchenne smile, and it has been described as "smiling with the eyes."

Proverbs reminds us that "a cheerful look brings joy to the heart" and "a cheerful heart is good medicine" (15:30 NLT; 17:22). Quite often, the smiles of God's children stem from the supernatural joy we possess. It's a gift from God that regularly spills out into our lives, as we encourage people who are carrying heavy burdens or share with those who are looking for answers to life's questions. Even when we experience suffering, our joy can still shine through.

When life seems dark, choose joy. Let your smile be a window of hope reflecting God's love and the light of His presence in your life.

The LORD is my strength and my shield; my heart trusts in him, and he helps me. My heart leaps for joy, and with my song I praise him. Psalm 28:7

We do this by keeping our eyes on Jesus, the champion who initiates and perfects our faith. Because of the joy awaiting him, he endured the cross, disregarding its shame. Now he is seated in the place of honor beside God's throne. Hebrews 12:2 NLT

A cheerful heart is good medicine. Proverbs 17:22

MOMENTS FOR RENEWAL

Ask God to restore an area of your life in which you feel drained or lifeless. Listen for His caring response to you.

75

The School of Pain

Read Psalm 119:65-80

I n his book *The Problem of Pain*, C. S. Lewis observes that "God whispers to us in our pleasures, speaks in our conscience, but shouts in our pains: it is His megaphone to rouse a deaf world." Suffering often helps us to redirect our focus. It shifts our thinking from immediate circumstances so that we can listen to God concerning His work in our lives. Life as usual is replaced by a spiritual schoolroom.

In the Old Testament, we read how the psalmist maintained a teachable heart even during painful circumstances. He accepted them as orchestrated by God, and in submission he prayed, "In faithfulness you have afflicted me" (Psalm 119:75). Isaiah the prophet viewed suffering as a refining process: "See, I have refined you, though not as silver; I have tested you in the furnace of affliction" (Isaiah 48:10). And Job, despite his laments, learned about the sovereignty and greatness of God through his troubles (Job 40–42).

We are not alone in our experience of pain. God himself took on human form and suffered greatly: "To this you were called, because Christ suffered for you, leaving you an example, that you should follow in his steps" (1 Peter 2:21). The One with nail-scarred hands is near. He will comfort us and teach us in our suffering.

MOMENTS FOR REFLECTION

In faithfulness you have afflicted me. Psalm 119:75

I have refined you, but not as silver is refined. Rather, I have refined you in the furnace of suffering.

Isaiah 48:10 NLT

You asked, "Who is this that questions my wisdom with such ignorance?" It is I—and I was talking about things I knew nothing about, things far too wonderful for me. Job 42:3 NLT

MOMENTS FOR RENEWAL

Father, I confess that I don't always see your purpose in my trials. Help me to trust you, and help me become more and more like you.

76

Hearing Us from Heaven

Read 1 Kings 8:37-45

At eighteen months old, little Maison had never heard his mother's voice. Then doctors fitted him with his first hearing aids and his mom, Lauryn, asked him, "Can you hear me?" The child's eyes lit up. "Hi, baby!" Lauryn added. A smiling Maison responded to his mother with soft coos. In tears, Lauryn knew she'd witnessed a miracle. She'd given birth to Maison prematurely after gunmen shot her three times during a random home invasion. Weighing just one pound, Maison spent 158 days in intensive care and wasn't expected to survive, let alone be able to hear.

That heartwarming story can remind us of the God who hears us. King Solomon prayed fervently for God's attuned ear, especially during troubling times. When "there is no rain" (1 Kings 8:35), during "famine or plague," disaster or disease (v. 37), war (v. 44), and even sin, "hear from heaven their prayer and their plea," Solomon prayed, "and uphold their cause" (v. 45).

In His goodness, God responded with a promise that still stirs our hearts. "If my people, who are called by my name, will humble themselves and pray and seek my face and turn from their wicked ways, then I will hear from heaven, and I will forgive their sin and will heal their land" (2 Chronicles 7:14). Heaven may seem a long way off. Yet Jesus is with those who believe in Him. God hears our prayers, and He answers them.

Hear from heaven their prayer and their plea.

1 Kings 8:45

Then if my people who are called by my name will humble themselves and pray and seek my face and turn from their wicked ways, I will hear from heaven and will forgive their sins and restore their land.

2 Chronicles 7:14 NLT

I am the LORD, who heals you. Exodus 15:26

MOMENTS FOR RENEWAL

Father, during my toughest struggles and troubles, I thank you for hearing my humble cry.

77

Imagine This!

Read Isaiah 65:17-25

During the course of a popular home renovation television program, viewers often hear the host say, "Imagine this!" Then she unveils what could be when old things are restored and drab walls and floors are painted or stained. In one episode, after the renovation the homeowner was so overjoyed that, along with other expressions of elation, the words "That's beautiful!" gushed from her lips three times.

One of the stunning "Imagine this!" passages in the Bible is Isaiah 65:17–25. What a dazzling re-creation scene! The future renovation of heaven and Earth is in view (v. 17), and it's not merely cosmetic. It's deep and real, life-altering and life-preserving. "They will build houses and dwell in them; they will plant vineyards and eat their fruit" (v. 21). Violence will be a thing of the past: "They will neither harm nor destroy on all my holy mountain" (v. 25).

While the reversals envisioned in Isaiah 65 will be realized in the future, the God who will orchestrate universal restoration is in the business of life change now. The apostle Paul assures us, "If anyone is in Christ, the new creation has come: The old has gone, the new is here!" (2 Corinthians 5:17). In need of restoration? Has your life been broken by doubt, disobedience, and pain? Life change through Jesus is real and beautiful and available to those who ask and believe.

MOMENTS FOR REFLECTION

See, I will create new heavens and a new earth. The former things will not be remembered. Isaiah 65:17

Look! God's dwelling place is now among the people, and he will dwell with them. They will be his people, and God himself will be with them and be their God. "He will wipe every tear from their eyes. There will be no more death" or mourning or crying or pain, for the old order of things has passed away. Revelation 21:3–4

Behold, all things have become new.

2 Corinthians 5:17 NKJV

MOMENTS FOR RENEWAL

Talk to God about an area of your life in which you struggle to see how He can bring restoration and healing. Listen for His loving response to you.

78

God's Love Is Stronger

Read Song of Songs 8:4-7

In 2020, Alyssa Mendoza received a surprising email from her father in the middle of the night. The message had instructions about what to do for her mother on her parents' twenty-fifth anniversary. Why was this shocking? Alyssa's father had passed away ten months earlier. She discovered that he'd written and scheduled the email while he was sick, knowing he might not be there. He'd also arranged and paid for flowers to be sent to his wife for upcoming years on her birthday, future anniversaries, and Valentine's Day.

This story could stand as an example of the kind of love that's described in detail in Song of Songs. "Love is as strong as death, its jealousy unyielding as the grave" (8:6). Comparing graves and death to love seems odd, but they're strong because they don't give up their captives. However, neither will true love give up the loved one. The book reaches its peak in verses 6–7, describing marital love as one so strong that "many waters cannot quench [it]" (v. 7).

Throughout the Bible, the love of a husband and wife is compared to God's love (Isaiah 54:5; Ephesians 5:25; Revelation 21:2). Jesus is the groom and the church is His bride. God showed His love for us by sending Christ to face death so we wouldn't have to die for our sins (John 3:16). Whether we're married or single, we can remember that God's love is stronger than anything we could imagine.

Put me like a seal over your heart, like a seal on your arm. For love is as strong as death, jealousy is as severe as Sheol; its flames are flames of fire. Song of Songs 8:6 NASB

For your Maker is your husband—the LORD Almighty is his name. Isaiah 54:5

I saw the holy city, the new Jerusalem, coming down from God out of heaven like a bride beautifully dressed for her husband. Revelation 21:2 NLT

MOMENTS FOR RENEWAL

Tell Jesus that you love Him. Listen for His heart for you.

79

The Ticking Watch

Read Psalm 37:1-7

A group of workers were cutting ice out of a frozen lake and storing it in an icehouse when one of them realized he'd lost his watch in the windowless building. He and his friends searched for it in vain.

After they gave up, a young boy who'd seen them exit went into the building. Soon, he emerged with the watch. Asked how he'd found it, he replied: "I just sat down and kept quiet, and soon I could hear it ticking."

The Bible talks much about the value of being still. And no wonder, for God sometimes speaks in a whisper (1 Kings 19:12). In the busyness of life, it can be hard to hear Him. But if we stop rushing about and spend some quiet time with Him and the Scriptures, we may hear His gentle voice in our thoughts.

Psalm 37:1–7 assures us that we can trust God to rescue us from the "wicked schemes" of evil people, give us refuge, and help us stay faithful. But how can we do this when turmoil is all around us?

Verse 7 suggests: "Be still before the LORD and wait patiently for him." We could start by learning to keep silent for a few minutes after prayer. Or by quietly reading the Bible and letting the words soak into our hearts. And then, perhaps, we'll hear His wisdom speaking to us, quiet and steady as a ticking watch.

> After the earthquake came a fire, but the LORD was not in the fire. And after the fire came a gentle whisper. 1 Kings 19:12

> Be still in the presence of the LORD, and wait patiently for him to act. Psalm 37:7 NLT

> Commit your way to the LORD, trust also in Him, and He shall bring it to pass. He shall bring forth your righteousness as the light, and your justice as the noonday. Psalm 37:5–6 NKJV

MOMENTS FOR RENEWAL

Father, quiet my heart, mind, and soul so that I might hear your gentle whisper in my life.

80

Our Divine Defense

Read Nehemiah 4:7-18

Under Nehemiah's supervision, the Israelite workers were re-building the wall around Jerusalem. When they were nearly half finished, however, they learned that their enemies were plotting to attack Jerusalem. This news demoralized the already exhausted workers.

Nehemiah had to do something. First, he prayed and posted numerous guards in strategic places. Then, he armed his workers. "Those who carried materials did their work with one hand and held a weapon in the other, and each of the builders wore his sword at his side as he worked" (Nehemiah 4:17–18).

We who are building God's kingdom need to arm ourselves against the attack of our spiritual enemy, Satan. Our protection is the sword of the Spirit, which is God's Word. Memorizing Scripture and meditating on it enable us to "take [our] stand against the devil's schemes" (Ephesians 6:11). If we think that working for God doesn't matter, we should turn to the promise that what we do for Jesus will last for eternity (1 Corinthians 3:11–15). If we fear we've sinned too greatly for God to use us, we must remember we've been forgiven by the power of Jesus's blood (Matthew 26:28). And if we're worried we might fail if we try to serve God, we can recall that Jesus said we will bear fruit as we abide in Him (John 15:5).

God's Word is our divine defense!

MOMENTS FOR REFLECTION

Take . . . the sword of the Spirit, which is the word of God. Ephesians 6:17

Even those who carried building materials worked with one hand and kept a weapon in the other, and everyone who was building kept a sword strapped to their waist. Nehemiah 4:17–18 GNT

For no one can lay any foundation other than the one we already have—Jesus Christ. Anyone who builds on that foundation may use a variety of materials—gold, silver, jewels, wood, hay, or straw. But on the judgment day, fire will reveal what kind of work each builder has done. The fire will show if a person's work has any value. 1 Corinthians 3:11–13 NLT

MOMENTS FOR RENEWAL

Father, your Word is alive and active. Please help me to remember it when I am worried or fearful, when I need encouragement and inspiration.

81

Shining the Light

Read Matthew 5:13–16

Stephen told his parents that he needed to get to school early every day, but for some reason he never explained why it was so important. Yet they made sure he arrived at Northview High School by 7:15 each morning.

On a wintry day during his junior year, Stephen was in a car accident that sadly took his life. Later, his mom and dad found out why he'd been going to school so early. Each morning he and some friends had gathered at the school entrance to greet other students with a smile, a wave, and a kind word. It made all students—even those who weren't popular—feel welcomed and accepted.

A believer in Jesus, Stephen wanted to share His joy with those who desperately needed it. His example lives on as a reminder that one of the best ways to shine the light of Christ's love is by gestures of kindness and through a welcoming spirit.

In Matthew 5:14–16, Jesus reveals that in Him we're "the light of the world" and "a town built on a hill" (v. 14). Ancient cities were often built of white limestone, truly standing out as they reflected the blazing sun. May we choose not to be hidden but to give light "to everyone in the house" (v. 15).

And as we "let [our] light shine before others" (v. 16), may they experience the welcoming love of Christ.

MOMENTS FOR REFLECTION

You are the light of the world. A town built on a hill cannot be hidden. Neither do people light a lamp and put it under a bowl. Instead they put it on its stand, and it gives light to everyone in the house. Matthew 5:14–15

Those who are wise will shine like the brightness of the heavens, and those who lead many to righteousness, like the stars for ever and ever. Daniel 12:3

He said to them, "Follow Me, and I will make you fishers of men." Matthew 4:19 NKJV

MOMENTS FOR RENEWAL

Ask the Holy Spirit how you could welcome someone who may be lonely or in need of help, and wait for His response.

82

Invisible Influence

Read 1 Thessalonians 5:16-24

The National Gallery of Art in Washington, DC, houses a masterpiece called *The Wind*. If you get a chance to visit the museum when it's on display, you can view the dynamic image of a storm striking a forest with its hurricane-like power: Pummeled by the wind streaming from one direction, tall, thin trees lean and swerve—alive with the wind's motion.

In an even more powerful sense, the Holy Spirit is able to sway believers in the direction of God's goodness and truth. If we go along with the Spirit, we can expect to become more courageous and more loving. We will also become more discerning about how to handle our desires (2 Timothy 1:7).

In some situations, however, the Spirit nudges us toward spiritual growth and change, but we respond with a no. Continually stonewalling this conviction is what Scripture calls "quench[ing] the Spirit" (1 Thessalonians 5:19). Over time, things we once considered wrong appear not to be quite as bad.

When our relationship with God seems distant and disconnected, this may be because the Spirit's conviction has been repeatedly brushed aside. The longer this goes on, the harder it is to see the root of the problem. Thankfully, we can pray and ask God to show us our sin. If we turn away from sin and recommit ourselves to Him, God will forgive us and revive the power and influence of His Spirit within us.

Do not quench the Spirit. 1 Thessalonians 5:19

For the Spirit God gave us does not make us timid, but gives us power, love and self-discipline. 2 Timothy 1:7

Eli told Samuel, "Go and lie down, and if he calls you, say, 'Speak, Lord, for your servant is listening.'" So Samuel went and lay down in his place. The Lord came and stood there, calling as at the other times, "Samuel! Samuel!" Then Samuel said, "Speak, for your servant is listening." 1 Samuel 3:9–10

MOMENTS FOR RENEWAL

Father, show me how I have resisted your Holy Spirit. Help me to listen when you speak. I want to be right with you again.

83

Navigating the Storms of Life

Read Psalm 43

On July 16, 1999, the small plane piloted by John F. Kennedy Jr. crashed into the Atlantic Ocean. Investigators determined the cause of the accident to be a common error known as spatial disorientation. This phenomenon occurs when, due to poor visibility, pilots become disoriented and forget to rely on their instruments to help them successfully reach their destination.

As we navigate life, there are often times when life gets so overwhelming we feel disoriented. A cancer diagnosis, the death of a loved one, a job loss, a betrayal by a friend—life's unexpected tragedies can easily leave us feeling lost and confused.

When we find ourselves in these kinds of situations, we might try offering the prayer of Psalm 43. In this psalm, the psalmist is overwhelmed and feeling lost because he feels surrounded by evil and injustice. In despair, the psalmist pleads with God to provide His sure guidance to help him safely navigate through the situation to his desired destination, God's presence (vv. 3–4). In God's presence the psalmist knows he'll find renewed hope and joy.

What are the tools the psalmist requests for guidance? The light of truth and the assurance of God's presence by His Holy Spirit.

When you're feeling disoriented and lost, God's faithful guidance through His Spirit and loving presence can comfort you and light your way.

MOMENTS FOR REFLECTION

Send me your light and your faithful care, let them lead me. Psalm 43:3

Teach us to number our days, that we may gain a heart of wisdom. Psalm 90:12 NKJV

Trust in the LORD with all your heart, and lean not on your own understanding; in all your ways acknowledge Him, and He shall direct your paths. Proverbs 3:5–6 NKJV

MOMENTS FOR RENEWAL

Father, thank you that you've not left me alone in the challenging and disorienting circumstances of life. Please help me to rely on you to guide my steps today.

84

Unexpected Change

Read James 4:13–17

In January 1943, warm Chinook winds hit Spearfish, South Dakota, quickly raising the temperatures from –4° to 45°F (–20° to 7°C). That drastic weather change—a swing of 49 degrees—took place in just two minutes. The widest temperature change recorded in the United States over a twenty-four-hour period is an incredible 103 degrees! On January 15, 1972, Loma, Montana, saw the temperature jump from –54° to 49°F (–48° to 9°C).

Sudden change, however, is not simply a weather phenomenon. It's sometimes the very nature of life. James reminds us, "Now listen, you who say, 'Today or tomorrow we will go to this or that city, spend a year there, carry on business and make money.' Why, you do not even know what will happen tomorrow" (4:13–14). An unexpected loss. A surprise diagnosis. A financial reversal. Sudden changes.

Life is a journey with many unpredictable elements. This is precisely why James warns us to turn from "arrogant schemes" (v. 16) that do not take the Almighty into account. As he advised us, "You ought to say, 'If it is the Lord's will, we will live and do this or that'" (v. 15). The events of our lives may be uncertain, but one thing is sure: through all of life's unexpected moments, our God will never leave us. He's our one constant throughout life.

Come now, you who say, "Today or tomorrow we will go to such and such a city, spend a year there, buy and sell, and make a profit"; whereas you do not know what will happen tomorrow. For what is your life?

James 4:13–14 NKJV

And the LORD, He is the One who goes before you. He will be with you, He will not leave you nor forsake you; do not fear nor be dismayed." Deuteronomy 31:8 NKJV

MOMENTS FOR RENEWAL

Father, forgive me for the times I worry over things I can't anticipate or control, and help me find my rest in you.

85

Sweet Reminders

Read Exodus 3:7-17

When the tomb of Egyptian King Tutankhamen was discovered in 1922, it was filled with things ancient Egyptians thought were needed in the afterlife. Among items such as golden shrines, jewelry, clothing, furniture, and weapons was a pot filled with honey—still edible after more than three thousand years! Today we think of honey primarily as a sweetener, but in the ancient world it had many other uses. Honey is one of the only foods known to have all the nutrients needed to sustain life, so it was eaten for nutrition. In addition, honey has medicinal value. It is one of the oldest known wound dressings because it has properties that prevent infection.

When God rescued the children of Israel from Egyptian captivity, He promised to lead them to a "land flowing with milk and honey" (Exodus 3:8, 17), a metaphor for abundance. When their journey was prolonged due to sin, God fed them bread (manna) that tasted like honey (16:31). The Israelites grumbled about having to eat the same food for so long, but it's likely that God was kindly reminding them of what they would enjoy in the promised land.

God still uses honey to remind us that His ways and words are sweeter than the honeycomb (Psalm 19:10). So then the words we speak should also be like the honey we eat—healing and sweet to the soul (Proverbs 16:24).

I have come down to rescue them from the power of the Egyptians and lead them out of Egypt into their own fertile and spacious land. It is a land flowing with milk and honey. Exodus 3:8 NLT

The people of Israel called the bread manna. It was white like coriander seed and tasted like wafers made with honey. Exodus 16:31

Gracious words are a honeycomb, sweet to the soul and healing to the bones. Proverbs 16:24

MOMENTS FOR RENEWAL

Ask God how you can encourage others and bring healing through your words and actions today. How does He respond?

86

The Picture of Despair

Read Psalm 107:4-9

During the Great Depression in the United States, photographer Dorothea Lange snapped a photo of Florence Owens Thompson and her children. This well-known photograph, *Migrant Mother*, is the picture of a mother's despair in the aftermath of the failed pea harvest. Lange took it in Nipomo, California, while working for the Farm Security Administration, hoping to make them aware of the needs of the desperate seasonal farm laborers.

The book of Lamentations presents another snapshot of despair—that of Judah in the wake of the destruction of Jerusalem. Before the army of Nebuchadnezzar swept in to destroy the city, the people had suffered from starvation thanks to a siege (2 Kings 24:10–11). Though their turmoil was the result of years of disobedience to God, the writer of Lamentations cried out to God on behalf of his people (Lamentations 2:11–12).

While the author of Psalm 107 also describes a desperate time in Israel's history (during Israel's wanderings in the wilderness, vv. 4–5), the focus shifts to an action step to be taken in hard times: "Then they cried out to the Lord in their trouble" (v. 6). And what a wonderful result: "he delivered them from their distress."

In despair? Don't stay silent. Cry out to God. He hears and waits to restore your hope. Though He doesn't always take us out of hard situations, He promises to be with us always.

> I have cried until the tears no longer come; my heart is broken. Lamentations 2:11 NLT

> You know what I long for, Lord; you hear my every sigh. Psalm 38:9 NLT

> Let them praise the LORD for his great love and for the wonderful things he has done for them. For he satisfies the thirsty and fills the hungry with good things. Psalm 107:8–9 NLT

MOMENTS FOR RENEWAL

Father, I'm grateful for your comforting presence—thank you for promising to be with me always.

87

Who Am I?

Read Exodus 3:7-15

ears ago, world-famous evangelist Billy Graham was scheduled to speak at Cambridge University in England, but he did not feel qualified to address the sophisticated thinkers. He had no advanced degrees, and he had never attended seminary. Billy confided in a close friend: "I do not know that I have ever felt more inadequate and totally unprepared for a mission." He prayed for God's help, and God used him to share the simple truth of the gospel and the cross of Christ.

Moses also felt inadequate when God recruited him for the task of telling Pharaoh to release the Israelites. Moses asked, "Who am I that I should go to Pharaoh?" (Exodus 3:11). Although Moses may have questioned his effectiveness because he was "slow of speech" (4:10), God said, "I will be with you" (3:12). Knowing he would have to share God's rescue plan and tell the Israelites who sent him, Moses asked God, "What shall I tell them?" God replied, "I Am has sent me to you" (vv. 13–14). His name, "I Am," revealed His eternal, self-existent, and all-sufficient character.

Even when we question our ability to do what God has asked us to do, He can be trusted. Our shortcomings are less important than God's sufficiency. When we ask, "Who am I?" we can remember that God said, "I Am."

> But Moses replied, "When I go to the Israelites and say to them, 'The God of your ancestors sent me to you,' they will ask me, 'What is his name?' So what can I tell them?"
>
> God said, "I am who I am. You must tell them: 'The one who is called I Am has sent me to you.'"
>
> Exodus 3:13–14 GNT

> I am telling you the truth," Jesus replied. "Before Abraham was born, 'I Am'." John 8:58 GNT

MOMENTS FOR RENEWAL

Father, even when I feel inadequate or ill-equipped, help me trust that you can empower me to do whatever task you ask of me.

88

A Flying Miracle

Read Psalm 104:10-24

Among God's creatures, the butterfly is one of the most stunningly beautiful! Its gentle flight, colorful wings, and amazing migratory patterns are traits that make the butterfly a masterpiece of the natural world.

This flying insect, while supplying us with visual enjoyment, also provides us with amazing examples of the marvels of God's creative work.

For instance, the majestic monarch butterfly can travel three thousand miles on its migration to Central America—only to end up at the same tree its parents or even grandparents landed on a generation or two earlier. It does this guided by a brain the size of a pinhead.

Or consider the monarch's metamorphosis. After the caterpillar builds a chrysalis around itself, it releases a chemical that turns its insides to mush—no perceptible parts. Somehow from this emerges the brain, internal parts, head, legs, and wings of a butterfly.

One butterfly expert said, "The creation of the body of a caterpillar into the body and wings of a butterfly is, without doubt, one of the wonders of life on earth." Another expert feels that this metamorphosis is "rightly regarded as a miracle."

"How many are [God's] works!" (Psalm 104:24)—and the butterfly is but one of them.

MOMENTS FOR REFLECTION

How many are your works, LORD! In wisdom you made them all; the earth is full of your creatures. There is the sea, vast and spacious, teeming with creatures beyond number—living things both large and small. Psalm 104:24–25

God looked at everything he had made, and he was very pleased. Genesis 1:31 GNT

He who made the Pleiades and Orion, who turns midnight into dawn and darkens day into night, who calls for the waters of the sea and pours them out over the face of the land—the LORD is his name. Amos 5:8

MOMENTS FOR RENEWAL

Ponder the works of God's creation and worship Him. Let Him respond to your praise.

89

Not Rushing Prayer

Read Psalm 46

Alice Kaholusuna recounts a story of how the Hawaiian people would sit outside their temples for a lengthy amount of time preparing themselves before entering in. Even after entering, they would creep to the altar to offer their prayers. Afterward, they would sit outside again for a long time to "breathe life" into their prayers. When missionaries came to the island, the Hawaiians sometimes considered their prayers odd. The missionaries would stand up, utter a few sentences, call them "prayer," say amen, and be done with it. The Hawaiians described these prayers as "without breath."

Alice's story speaks of how God's people may not always take the opportunity to "be still, and know" (Psalm 46:10). Make no mistake—God hears our prayers, whether they're quick or slow. But often the pace of our lives mimics the pace of our hearts, and we need to allow ample time for God to speak into not only our lives but the lives of those around us. How many life-giving moments have we missed by rushing, saying amen, and being done with it?

We're often impatient with everything from slow people to the slow lane in traffic. Yet, God in His kindness says, "Be still. Breathe in and out. Go slow, and remember that I am God, your refuge and strength, an ever-present help in trouble." To do so is to know that God is God. To do so is to trust. To do so is to live.

MOMENTS FOR REFLECTION

Be still, and know that I am God. Psalm 46:10

Then a great and powerful wind tore the mountains apart and shattered the rocks before the LORD, but the LORD was not in the wind. After the wind there was an earthquake, but the LORD was not in the earthquake. After the earthquake came a fire, but the LORD was not in the fire. And after the fire came a gentle whisper. 1 Kings 19:11–12

MOMENTS FOR RENEWAL

Father, thank you for being my ever-present help in any situation. Give me the grace to be still and know that you're God.

90

Every Word Matters

Read Deuteronomy 4:1–10

Kim Peek was a savant (a person with extraordinary memory) who memorized all of Shakespeare's plays. During a performance of *Twelfth Night*, Peek noticed that the actor had skipped a word from one of the lines. Peek suddenly stood up and shouted, "Stop!" The actor apologized and said he didn't think anyone would mind. Peek replied, "Shakespeare would."

Words matter. But especially when they are the very words of God. Moses warned Israel, "Do not add to what I command you and do not subtract from it, but keep the commands of the Lord your God that I give you" (Deuteronomy 4:2). Moses often reminded Israel of God's mercy and faithfulness to them in the past. But he also stressed the importance of obedience to God's commands as they prepared to enter the promised land. He told them that obedience would result in blessings of life and a rich inheritance (vv. 39–40). Every command and regulation mattered to God. The value His people placed on God's Word showed their view of Him.

Today, when we value God's Word, handle it with great care, and obey what it says, we give God the reverence He truly deserves.

MOMENTS FOR REFLECTION

Do not add to what I command you and do not subtract from it, but keep the commands of the LORD your God that I give you. Deuteronomy 4:2

Therefore, everyone who hears these words of Mine, and acts on them, will be like a wise man who built his house on the rock. Matthew 7:24 NASB

Your word is a lamp to my feet and a light to my path. Psalm 119:105 NKJV

MOMENTS FOR RENEWAL

Father, help me to treasure every part of your Word and to listen to its wisdom.

91

How to Stay on Track

Read 1 John 2:18-27

As the world's fastest blind runner, David Brown of the United States Paralympic Team credits his wins to God, his mother's early advice ("no sitting around"), and his running guide—veteran sprinter Jerome Avery. Tethered to Brown by a string tied to their fingers, Avery guides Brown's winning races with words and touches.

"It's all about listening to his cues," says Brown, who says he could "swing out wide" on two hundred-meter races where the track curves. "Day in and day out, we're going over race strategies," Brown says, "communicating with each other—not only verbal cues, but physical cues."

In our own life's race, we're blessed with a Divine Guide. Our Helper, the Holy Spirit, leads our steps when we follow Him. "I am writing these things to you about those who are trying to lead you astray," wrote John (1 John 2:26). "But you have received the Holy Spirit, and he lives within you, so you don't need anyone to teach you what is true. For the Spirit teaches you everything you need to know" (v. 27 NLT).

John stressed this wisdom to the believers of his day who faced "antichrists" who denied the Father and that Jesus is the Messiah (v. 22). We face such deniers today as well. But the Holy Spirit, our Guide, leads us in following Jesus. We can trust His guidance to touch us with truth, keeping us on track.

MOMENTS FOR REFLECTION

The Spirit teaches you everything you need to know, and what he teaches is true—it is not a lie. 1 John 2:27 NLT

May the God of hope fill you with all joy and peace as you trust in him, so that you may overflow with hope by the power of the Holy Spirit. Romans 15:13

I will ask the Father, and he will give you another Advocate, who will never leave you. John 14:16 NLT

MOMENTS FOR RENEWAL

Father, attune my heart to your Holy Spirit's guidance so that I'll run to your truth and not to lies.

92

Prayerful Wrestling

Read Genesis 32:24-32

Dennis's life was transformed after someone gave him a New Testament. Reading it captivated him, and it became his constant companion. Within six months, two life-changing events occurred in his life. He placed his faith in Jesus for the forgiveness of his sins, and he was diagnosed with a brain tumor after experiencing severe headaches. Because of the unbearable pain, he became bedridden and unable to work. One painful, sleepless night he found himself crying out to God. Sleep finally came at 4:30 a.m.

Bodily pain can cause us to cry out to God, but other excruciating life circumstances also compel us to run to Him. Centuries before Dennis's night of wrestling, a desperate Jacob faced off with God (Genesis 32:24–32). For Jacob, it was unfinished family business. He had wronged his brother Esau (Genesis 27), and he feared that payback was imminent. In seeking God's help in this difficult situation, Jacob encountered God face to face (32:30) and emerged from it a changed man.

And so did Dennis. After pleading with God in prayer, Dennis was able to stand up after being bedridden, and the doctor's examination showed no signs of the tumor. Although God doesn't always choose to miraculously heal us, we're confident that He hears our prayers and will give us what we need for our situation. In our desperation we offer sincere prayers to God and leave the results to Him!

MOMENTS FOR REFLECTION

Jacob was left alone, and a man wrestled with him till daybreak. Genesis 32:24

Jacob named the place Peniel (which means "face of God"), for he said, "I have seen God face to face, yet my life has been spared." Genesis 32:30 NLT

My God, my God, why have you forsaken me? . . . Yet you brought me out of the womb; you made me trust in you, even at my mother's breast. From birth I was cast on you; from my mother's womb you have been my God. Psalm 22:1, 9–10

MOMENTS FOR RENEWAL

Talk to God about an area in which you are struggling, and listen to His heart for you.

93

Are You Hungry Now?

Read James 2:14–18

Thomas knew what he needed to do. Having been born to a poor family in India and adopted by Americans, upon a return trip to India he witnessed the dire needs of the children in his hometown. So he knew he had to help. He began making plans to return to the United States, finish his education, save a lot of money, and come back in the future.

Then, after reading James 2:14–18 in which James asks, "What good is it . . . if someone claims to have faith but has no deeds?" Thomas heard a little girl in his native country cry out to her mother: "But Mommy, I'm hungry now!" He was reminded of the times he had been intensely hungry as a child—searching through trash cans for food. Thomas knew he couldn't wait years to help. He decided, "I'll start now!"

Today the orphanage he began houses fifty well-fed and cared for children who are learning about Jesus and getting an education—all because one man didn't put off what he knew God was asking him to do.

James's message applies to us as well. Our faith in Jesus Christ provides us with great advantages—a relationship with Him, an abundant life, and a future hope. But what good is it doing anyone else if we don't reach out and help those in need? Can you hear the cry: "I'm hungry now?"

What good is it, my brothers and sisters, if someone claims to have faith but has no deeds?. . . Faith by itself, if it is not accompanied by action, is dead. James 2:14, 17

If you help the poor, you are lending to the LORD—and he will repay you! Proverbs 19:17 NLT

Do not forget to do good and to share with others, for with such sacrifices God is pleased. Hebrews 13:16

MOMENTS FOR RENEWAL

Reflect on the needs that move you to compassion, and ask God how He is calling you to respond.

94

A House on a Rock

Read Matthew 7:24-29

As many as thirty-four thousand homes in one US state are at risk of collapsing due to faulty foundations. Without realizing it, a concrete company pulled stone from a quarry laced with a mineral that, over time, causes concrete to crack and disintegrate. The foundations of nearly six hundred homes have already crumbled, and that number will likely skyrocket over time.

Jesus used the image of building a home atop a faulty foundation to explain the far riskier danger of building our lives on unsteady ground. He explained how some of us construct our life on sturdy rock, ensuring that we hold solid when we face fierce storms. Others of us, however, erect our lives on sand; and when the tempests rage, our lives tumble "with a great crash" (Matthew 7:27). The one distinction between building on an unshakable foundation and a crumbling one is whether or not we put Christ's words "into practice" (v. 26). The question isn't whether or not we hear His words, but whether we practice them as He enables us.

There's much wisdom offered to us in this world—plus lots of advice and help—and much of it is good and beneficial. If we base our life on any foundation other than humble obedience to God's truth, however, we invite trouble. In His strength, doing what God says is the only way to have a house, a life, built on rock.

Everyone who hears these words of mine and puts them into practice is like a wise man who built his house on the rock. Matthew 7:24

If you need wisdom, ask our generous God, and he will give it to you. He will not rebuke you for asking. James 1:5 NLT

For the LORD gives wisdom; from his mouth come knowledge and understanding. Proverbs 2:6

MOMENTS FOR RENEWAL

Father, so much of what I experience feels unsteady and temporary, a life built on sand. I want to build my life on you and your wisdom. Help me to listen and respond to your promptings today.

95

Surrendering All

Read Mark 10:26–31

Two men remembered for serving others for Jesus left careers in the arts to commit themselves to where they believed God had called them. James O. Fraser (1886–1938) decided not to pursue being a concert pianist in England to serve the Lisu people in China, while the American Judson Van DeVenter (1855–1939) chose to become an evangelist instead of pursuing a career in art. He later wrote the hymn "I Surrender All."

While having a vocation in the arts is the perfect calling for many, these men believed God called them to relinquish one career for another. Perhaps they found inspiration from Jesus counseling the rich, young ruler to give up his possessions to follow Him (Mark 10:17–25). Witnessing the exchange, Peter exclaimed, "We have left everything to follow you!" (v. 28). Jesus assured him that God would give those who follow Him "a hundred times as much in this present age" and eternal life (v. 30). But He would give according to His wisdom: "Many who are first will be last, and the last first" (v. 31).

No matter where God has placed us, we're called to daily surrender our lives to Christ, obeying His gentle call to follow Him and serve Him with our talents and resources—whether in the home, office, community, or far from home.

"Truly I tell you," Jesus replied, "no one who has left home or brothers or sisters or mother or father or children or fields for me and the gospel will fail to receive a hundred times as much in this present age: homes, brothers, sisters, mothers, children and fields—along with persecutions—and in the age to come eternal life." Mark 10:29–30

Therefore, I urge you, brothers and sisters, in view of God's mercy, to offer your bodies as a living sacrifice, holy and pleasing to God—this is your true and proper worship. Romans 12:1

Still other seed fell on good soil, where it produced a crop—a hundred, sixty or thirty times what was sown. Matthew 13:8

MOMENTS FOR RENEWAL

Ask God if there's an area of your life that He wants you to surrender more fully to Him. Listen for His response—and His heart—toward you.

96

Of Prayer
and Dust and Stars

Read Genesis 15:1-6

Lara and Dave desperately wanted a baby, but their physician told them they were unable to have one. Lara confided to a friend: "I found myself having some very honest talks with God." But it was after one of those "talks" that she and Dave spoke to their pastor, who told them about an adoption ministry at their church. A year later they were blessed with an adopted baby boy.

In Genesis 15, the Bible tells of another honest conversation—this one between Abram and God. God had told him, "Do not be afraid, Abram. I am . . . your very great reward" (v. 1). But Abram, uncertain of God's promises about his future, answered candidly: "Sovereign LORD, what can you give me since I remain childless?" (v. 2).

Earlier God had promised Abram, "I will make your offspring like the dust of the earth" (13:16). Now Abram—in a very human moment—reminded God of that. But note God's response: He assured Abram by telling him to look up and "count the stars—if indeed you can," indicating his descendants would be beyond numbering (15:5).

How good is God, not only to allow such candid prayer but also to gently reassure Abram! Later, God would change his name to Abraham ("father of many"). Like Abraham, you and I can openly share our hearts with Him and know that we can trust Him to do what's best for us and others.

MOMENTS FOR REFLECTION

"Look up at the sky and count the stars—if indeed you can count them." Then he said to him, "So shall your offspring be." Genesis 15:5

And so a whole nation came from this one man who was as good as dead—a nation with so many people that, like the stars in the sky and the sand on the seashore, there is no way to count them. Hebrews 11:12 NLT

MOMENTS FOR RENEWAL

Father, thank you for caring about even the most intimate details of my life. Help me to stay close to you in prayer today.

97

Hearing God

Read 1 Samuel 3:1–10

Have you ever had a cold where you struggled to hear clearly? Your symptoms began muffling and muting sounds, and you almost felt as if you were living underwater? Until we experience a situation where we lose our hearing, it's easy to take it for granted.

Young Samuel in the temple must have wondered what he was hearing as he struggled out of sleep at the summons of his name (1 Samuel 3:4). Three times he presented himself before Eli, the high priest. Only the third time did Eli realize it was the Lord speaking to Samuel. The word of the Lord had been rare at that time (v. 1), and the people were not in tune with His voice. But Eli instructed Samuel how to respond (v. 9).

The Lord speaks much more now than in the days of Samuel. The letter to the Hebrews tells us, "In the past God spoke to our ancestors through the prophets . . . but in these last days he has spoken to us by his Son" (1:1–2). And in Acts 2 we read of the coming of the Holy Spirit at Pentecost (vv. 1–4), who guides us in the things Christ taught us (John 16:13). But we need to learn to hear His voice and respond in obedience. We may hear as if underwater, as we would when afflicted by a bad cold or flu. We need to test what we think is the Lord's guidance with the Bible and with other mature Christians.

As God's beloved children, we do hear His voice. He loves to speak life into us.

> In those days the word of the LORD was rare; there were not many visions. . . . Then the LORD called Samuel. Samuel answered, "Here I am." 1 Samuel 3:1, 4

> Suddenly a sound like the blowing of a violent wind came from heaven and filled the whole house where they were sitting. They saw what seemed to be tongues of fire that separated and came to rest on each of them. All of them were filled with the Holy Spirit and began to speak in other tongues as the Spirit enabled them. Acts 2:2–4

MOMENTS FOR RENEWAL

Say to God, "Speak, for I am listening" (see 1 Samuel 3:9). Listen for God's loving response.

98

Recovering What's Lost

Read 1 Samuel 30:1-6, 18-19

At the phone store, the young pastor steeled himself for bad news. His smartphone, accidentally dropped during class, was a total loss, right? Actually, no. The store clerk recovered all of the pastor's data, including his Bible videos and photos. She also recovered "every photo I'd ever deleted," he said. The store also "replaced my broken phone with a brand-new phone." As he said, "I recovered all I had lost and more."

David once led his own recovery mission after an attack by the vicious Amalekites. Spurned by Philistine rulers, David and his army discovered the Amalekites had raided and burned down their town of Ziklag—taking captive "the women and everyone else in it," including all their wives and children (1 Samuel 30:2–3). "So David and his men wept aloud until they had no strength left to weep" (v 4). The soldiers were so bitter with their leader David that they talked of "stoning him" (v. 6).

"But David found strength in the LORD his God" (v. 6). As God promised, David pursued the Amalekites and "recovered everything the Amalekites had taken. . . . Nothing was missing: young or old, boy or girl, plunder or anything else they had taken. David brought everything back" (vv. 18–19). As we face spiritual attacks that "rob" us even of hope, may we find renewed strength in God. He will be with us in every challenge of life.

MOMENTS FOR REFLECTION

But David found strength in the LORD his God.

David recovered everything the Amalekites had taken, including his two wives. Nothing was missing: young or old, boy or girl, plunder or anything else they had taken. David brought everything back.
1 Samuel 30:18–19

I cling to you; your right hand upholds me. Psalm 63:8

MOMENTS FOR RENEWAL

Father, I take refuge in you even as I face life's challenges. Please help me today.

99

Loving Others with Our Prayers

Read 2 Corinthians 1:8-11

*A*re people still praying for me?"

That was one of the first questions a missionary asked his wife whenever she was allowed to visit him in prison. He had been falsely accused and incarcerated for his faith for two years. His life was frequently in danger because of the conditions and hostility in the prison, and believers around the world were earnestly praying for him. He wanted to be assured they wouldn't stop, because he believed God was using their prayers in a powerful way.

Our prayers for others—especially those who are persecuted for their faith—are a vital gift. Paul made this clear when he wrote the believers in Corinth about hardships he faced during his missionary journey. He was "under great pressure," so much that he "despaired of life itself" (2 Corinthians 1:8). But then he told them God had delivered him and described the tool He'd used to do it: "We have set our hope that he will continue to deliver us, *as you help us by your prayers*" (vv. 10–11, emphasis added).

God moves through our prayers to accomplish great good in the lives of His people. One of the best ways to love others is to pray for them, because through our prayers we open the door to the help only God can provide. When we pray for others, we love them in His strength. There's none greater or more loving than He.

MOMENTS FOR REFLECTION

> This happened that we might not rely on ourselves but on God, who raises the dead. 2 Corinthians 1:9

> Don't worry about anything; instead, pray about everything. Tell God what you need, and thank him for all he has done. Then you will experience God's peace, which exceeds anything we can understand. His peace will guard your hearts and minds as you live in Christ Jesus. Philippians 4:6–7 NLT

> Pray in the Spirit at all times and on every occasion. Stay alert and be persistent in your prayers for all believers everywhere. Ephesians 6:18 NLT

MOMENTS FOR RENEWAL

Intercede for someone you know, asking God to guide you in advocating for him or her.

100

Freed from Our Cage

Read Psalm 18:3–6, 16–19

While out taking walks, writer Martin Laird would often encounter a man with four Kerry Blue Terriers. Three of the dogs ran wild through the open fields, but one stayed near its owner, running in tight circles. When Laird finally stopped and asked about this odd behavior, the owner explained that it was a rescue dog that had spent most of his life locked in a cage. The terrier continued to run in circles as though contained inside a confined box.

The Scriptures reveal that we're trapped and hopeless unless God rescues us. The psalmist spoke of being afflicted by an enemy, entrapped by "the snares of death" with the "cords of death . . . coiled around" him (Psalm 18:4–5). Enclosed and shackled, he cried to God for help (v. 6). And with thundering power, He "reached down . . . and took hold" of him (v. 16).

God can do the same for us. He can break the chains and release us from our confining cages. He can set us free and carry us "out into a spacious place" (v. 19). How sad it is, then, when we keep running in small circles, as if we're still confined in our old prisons. In His strength, may we no longer be bound by fear, shame, or oppression. God has rescued us from those cages of death. We can run free.

MOMENTS FOR REFLECTION

[God] brought me out into a spacious place; he rescued me because he delighted in me. Psalm 18:19

All of us, like sheep, have strayed away. We have left God's paths to follow our own. Yet the LORD laid on him the sins of us all. Isaiah 53:6 NLT

If the Son sets you free, you are truly free. John 8:36 NLT

MOMENTS FOR RENEWAL

Father, unbind me in any area in which I'm spiritually chained, and where I've been healed but still live as if I'm in bondage, help me realize that you've set me free!

CONTRIBUTORS

James Banks
John Blase
Dave Branon
Con Campbell
Anne Cetas
Peter W. Chin
Winn Collier
Bill Crowder
Mart DeHaan
Xochitl Dixon
Dennis Fisher
Tim Gustafson
Kirsten Holmberg
Arthur Jackson
Cindy Hess Kasper
Alyson Kieda
Leslie Koh
Monica La Rose
Julie Ackerman Link

David McCasland
Elisa Morgan
Remi Oyedele
Amy Peterson
Amy Boucher Pye
Patricia Raybon
David H. Roper
Lisa M. Samra
Jennifer Benson Schuldt
Julie Schwab
Sheridan Voysey
Linda Washington
Marvin Williams

To learn more about the writers of *Our Daily Bread*, visit odb.org/all-authors.

GENERAL EDITOR

Anna Haggard is associate content editor for Our Daily Bread Publishing. A follower of Jesus, she loves to write and edit books sharing about God's generous, deep love for all people. Anna coauthored the Called and Courageous Girls series, and she lives in Grand Rapids, Michigan.